THE
LATINO
ADVANTAGE
IN THE
WORKPLACE

THE LATINO ADVANTAGE IN THE WORKPLACE

USE WHO YOU ARE TO GET WHERE YOU WANT TO BE

Mariela Dabbah
Arturo Poiré

SPHINX® PUBLISHING
AN IMPRINT OF SOURCEBOOKS, INC.®
NAPERVILLE, ILLINOIS
www.SphinxLegal.com

First Edition: 2006

Published by: Sphinx® Publishing, An Imprint of Sourcebooks, Inc.®

Naperville Office
P.O. Box 4410
Naperville, Illinois 60567-4410
630-961-3900
Fax: 630-961-2168
www.sourcebooks.com
www.SphinxLegal.com

This publication is designed to provide accurate and authoritative information in regard to the
subject matter covered. It is sold with the understanding that the publisher is not engaged in
rendering legal, accounting, or other professional service. If legal advice or other expert assistance
is required, the services of a competent professional person should be sought.

*From a Declaration of Principles Jointly Adopted by a Committee of the
American Bar Association and a Committee of Publishers and Associations*

This product is not a substitute for legal advice.

Disclaimer required by Texas statutes.

Library of Congress Cataloging-in-Publication Data
Dabbah, Mariela.
  The Latino advantage in the workplace : use who you are to get where you
want to be / by Mariela Dabbah and Arturo Poiré. -- 1st ed.
    p. cm.
  ISBN-13: 978-1-57248-569-3 (pbk. : alk. paper)
  ISBN-10: 1-57248-569-8 (pbk. : alk. paper)
  1. Success in business--United States. 2. Hispanic Americans--Life skills
guides. 3. Hispanic American businesspeople. I. Poiré, Arturo. II. Title.

HF5386.D16 2006
650.1089'68073--dc22

                                                          2006026457

Printed and bound in the United States of America.
SB — 10 9 8 7 6 5 4 3 2 1

DEDICATION

To my siblings Fernando and Paula
M.D.

To Soledad
A.P.

Acknowledgments

We would like to thank Dianne Wheeler for her immediate interest in the book and Michael Bowen, our editor, for his visionary instincts and support through the publication process.

Our gratitude also goes to the colleagues and close friends who have supported us throughout the project and who read our manuscript to provide feedback: Ezequiel Caride, Marisol González, Susan Landon, Soledad Matteozzi, and Elizabeth Nieto.

We are deeply in debt to the many people who we interviewed for this book and who so openly shared their stories. We would like to specifically thank those who we profiled given the extent of the interview: Mario Bósquez, Esteban Creste, Cecilia Gutiérrez, Ernesto Schweikert, Teresa Mlawer, Lillian Ortiz, and Ana Duarte-McCarthy.

We thank Julie Stav from the bottom of our hearts for her ongoing mentorship and support, and for a wonderful foreword.

We extend our gratitude to the National Association of Hispanic Journalists (NAHJ) and its members for having welcomed us so warmly.

CONTENTS

    This is Your Club–Take Advantage of It
    How to Read this Book

PART I—LAYING THE FOUNDATION

    The Battle to Belong
    Maximizing Opportunities
    A Word about the Exercises
    Using Your Language
    Uniformity vs. Diversity

    Stereotypes and the Battle for Balance

PART II—THE LATINO ADVANTAGES

PART III—IMPROVEMENT OPPORTUNITIES

The Three Ps
Communication

Chapter 8: Networking
Who is a Contact?
Basic Rules
Great Places to Network
Networking in Practice

PART IV—BRINGING IT ALL TOGETHER

Epilogue

Appendix A: Directory of Resources

Appendix B: Let's Practice

Index

About the Authors

FOREWORD

In the past few years, the American publishing industry has seen a substantial growth in the number of all kinds of books focused on Latino subjects, another proof of our increasing contribution to and success in this country. With enormous satisfaction, we now see displayed in bookstores from coast to coast, titles on Latino cuisine, our countries, our habits, our artists, and our history. There are books that help with the citizenship exam and books to learn English or Spanish, titles on finances and relationships, novels by our best authors, and career manuals. Books for people to know us better and for us to learn how to better integrate into society in general.

Up until now, however, we didn't have a book like the one Mariela Dabbah and Arturo Poiré—two successful Latino authors who are an example of everything we can achieve when we set out to pursue our dreams—are making available to us. I don't think there is a book similar to *The Latino Advantage in the Workplace* out there, one so capable of showing us in a concrete, positive, entertaining, and realistic way the enormous wealth that our language, our character, our culture, our essence can offer us. A book that teaches us how to use this marvelous treasure to achieve our highest goals.

The Latino Advantage in the Workplace shows the reader, in a way no other book has been able to do up to now, *how to use who you are to get where you want to be,* as the subtitle promises. And it does it in an innovative way—through practical exercises taken from real-life situations. These exercises will enable us not only to discover and make use of our strong points, but also to recognize and tone down traits that could be an obstacle in our path to success in our personal or professional life. In my own experience as a financial planner and in my daily conversations with the thousands of listeners of my radio program, I've seen how difficult it could sometimes be for many Hispanics to take advantage of the incredible resources they have within their reach and of the many opportunities that could help them move up in life with more self-assurance.

Mariela and Arturo have elaborated a unique methodology that will help us succeed in our fight to become an integral part of this society and to overcome those barriers which, many times, we create ourselves. I don't think there is another title available to readers at the present time that will teach them with such precision and objectivity—you won't find here rhetoric like: "We are Latinos, and that's why we are better than the rest of you!"—how to maximize their potential; how to really understand what it means to belong, now and here in this country, to such a fast-moving and rich culture as ours; how to defeat any obstacles that may inhibit us from advancing further in order for us to become success stories like the ones we will read about in these pages.

The Latino Advantage in the Workplace tells you: "You are Latino and because of it you own a wonderful set of resources that can be used to attain a life in the United States that will be full of rewards. These are your virtues! Take advantage of them. These are your limitations! Overcome them." Through exercises and easy-to-implement activities, you will be able to value and use in your daily life the enormous power that your language, your culture, and your uniqueness provide you.

I felt very proud of Mariela Dabbah and Arturo Poiré when I read this book because they have discovered and shared a fantastic secret that, for the first time, will allow us to understand what it means to be a Latino and how to take advantage of a unique heritage and culture that will help us conquer the American Dream.

—Julie Stav

PREFACE

When we set out to write this book, our goal was to offer some useful tools to everyone with a Latino background, whether they were born in Latin America or into a Latino family in the United States. ("Latino" is being used to describe anyone whose heritage belongs to the Latin and South American region. While the term "Hispanic" is also commonly used and technically includes people born in Spain, both terms are used interchangeably.) The idea behind it is that we share certain cultural traits that have become innate to who we are as a people. By becoming aware of those characteristics we can use them to our advantage in order to advance our careers. Following the same logic, we can keep any shortcomings at bay. It is all about finding the right balance so that we can be ourselves and at the same time succeed in the American market.

We would like to make it clear that by no means do we pretend to say that all of the traits we talk about here are exclusively Latino. We would be falling prey to the same stereotypes we are trying to help you dispel. Many of the traits are present in various degrees in other groups and sometimes more in men than in women or vice versa. It is a good reminder that we are all people and that we have more in common than we have differences. Nonetheless, generalizations are necessary whenever you are studying a particular group and we find that the general statements we make throughout this book are justified in the name of helping readers understand certain behaviors.

Although there are many positive traits that work well in the American system, we have chosen the ones that we think will give you the biggest edge. After reading this book, you will be in good shape to think about other ones that can give you an even bigger edge.

Given that we all have slightly different backgrounds, you may not see yourself reflected in every trait we describe. Just take what you can use, practice the exercises that are meaningful to your situation, and move on. There is plenty of material in the book to satisfy your curiosity about yourself and your roots, and to help you advance in your career path.

We would also like to clarify here that we use the terms "United States" and "America" interchangeably, even though Latin America is part of the American continent. In addition, when we talk about "Americans," we refer to the Anglo-Saxon population of the U.S., to distinguish it from people with a Latino background, although many Latinos are American citizens.

One last note: the examples we use throughout the book are based on our experience and interviews with a large number of people. Many of these examples are a composite of several anecdotes that were then adapted to the topics of the book. The names we used are all fictional except for the ones featured in the profiles at the end of each chapter.

INTRODUCTION

Something is happening in the social environment of the United States. During the past ten years, there has been a noticeable change in American perceptions of Latinos and in the way in which this population has moved up the social ladder. When we first arrived in the U.S. many years ago, to be Latino was a different story.

During Arturo's first weeks at work in a large financial institution, Janet, one of his colleagues, scheduled a group meeting. The day of the meeting, Janet stopped by Arturo's cubicle to confirm that he was going to be there at the agreed time.

"Yes, sure. I'll see you there," he said.

She looked at him intently and asked, "Will you be there on time or on 'Latino' time?"

Arturo remembers feeling quite offended and he showed it in his facial expression. Janet noticed and apologized.

Mariela's first experience with the *Latino time* stereotype was with some American acquaintances. They invited her to a party on Saturday night at 7:00 p.m. When she arrived, she not only noticed that she was the first one but that nobody arrived for another hour. She soon learned that her friends had given her a different time, thinking she would be an hour late.

At the time, we could not help but wonder about other perceptions our friends and colleagues might have of us just because of where we came from. We each decided that in moving forward we would be very careful not to reinforce those stereotypes; we would learn the *American way,* and moreover, we would try and show the added value we brought to the table because of our origin.

Many things have changed in this past decade. Not only have Latinos become the largest minority in the U.S., but our growth and popularity seem to be unstoppable. From trends in music, entertainment, fashion, and food to the world of politics (where politicians from right and left are eager to attract Latinos), nowadays everything Latino is seen in a much more positive light.

That is how the idea for this book came about. During our time in the U.S. we have become increasingly convinced that the reasons for Latino success lie in our particular upbringing and cultural heritage. No matter what country our family comes from in Latin America, there are some traits and values that we all share and that make us particularly successful in this system. We all share stories of sacrifice and instability in the countries we left, and a dream to make the most out of the experience in our new homes.

This book will show you that there is a Latino advantage. That advantage comes from the traits and skills you have that can help you succeed in the American system in two ways.

1) We will look at the way we relate to each other, how we communicate, how we pursue our goals, and the importance we give to family and relationships. Through this we can make the most of the Latino advantage.

2) We will look at certain traits that need to be kept in check. These are characteristics that can easily reinforce some people's negative stereotypes of Latinos and can have an impact on our success.

The focus throughout the book will be on helping you succeed in America. We want to make sure you maximize your potential by effectively using what you bring from your heritage.

THIS IS YOUR CLUB—
TAKE ADVANTAGE OF IT

For those of you who may not be aware of the magnitude of this group, we have gathered some interesting statistics about the Latino population in the U.S.

- There are an estimated 41 million Latinos residing in the U.S., with a projection of 48 million for the year 2010 and 60 million for 2020. Of these 41 million, around 18 million speak Spanish at home. (Source: U.S. Census Bureau)
- U.S. Hispanic purchasing power has surged to nearly $700 billion and is projected to reach as much as $1 trillion by 2007, nearly three times the overall national rate over the past decade. (Source: HispanTelligence®)
- There are approximately two million Hispanic-owned businesses in the country that generate almost $300 billion in annual gross receipts. (Sources: Small Business Administration, HispanTelligence®)
- For 2003, the 500 largest Hispanic-owned firms in the country reported record revenues of $26.3 billion, an increase of 13.9% from the previous year. (Source: HispanTelligence®)

This data confirms what you might already suspect. Every trend indicates that the Latino community is making the best out of the American dream—and the future looks even brighter!

Add to this information the recent emphasis that companies are placing on diversity, and it is clear that there will be plenty of opportunities for continued and sustained improvement. Keep in mind, however, that diversity does not mean you will get preferential treatment; rather, you need to demonstrate that your diverse background translates into added value. This is exactly what our book is about.

How to Read this Book

There are many ways of reading this book, depending on your particular interests and level of self-knowledge. The obvious one is to read it cover to cover, but there are also plenty other ways that can be effective as well. We discuss some of them here so that you can compare and choose the one that suits you the best.

Each chapter is made up of several items.
- Theoretical material, where we describe each trait, discuss its connection with our heritage and its origin, and point out its impact on our lives in America
- Examples, where we use real-life situations to drive a point home
- Let's Practice sections, where we ask you to reflect on a specific situation or practice a skill we discussed
- Career Tips, where we provide more specific career applications of the different topics
- A profile of a successful Latino, where we showcase a person who has used his or her Latino Advantage with great success

Keeping all these elements in mind, here are a few possible ways in which you could take advantage of this text.
- You may decide to read the theoretical material and examples first, and do the activities later. However, we do not particularly recommend this approach, as we think that the activities are essential in learning how to maximize your abilities.
- You may read the Career Tips before you read a chapter (or even the book) so you get the raw application of what is discussed in the book. Afterwards you can read the rest. This approach has the advantage of giving you immediate satisfaction, as these tips are designed to have an impact regardless of your understanding of all the concepts in the book.

- You may choose which chapters are more interesting to you and read those first, although we do suggest that you read the first chapter before you go into any of the others, as it sets the groundwork for the remaining of the book. This approach might work for you if you already know which areas you need to focus on more urgently or need additional practice with.
- You may wish to read the profiles for inspiration before you read a chapter. Keep in mind that we have selected very real people, in the sense that it will be easy to identify with their situations and learn from how they took advantage of their innate Latino traits.

Any way you choose to read *The Latino Advantage in the Workplace*, we would like to think that there is a before and an after you read this book. You will walk away with a lot of practical and useful information that you can apply immediately.

Happy journey!

PART 1

LAYING THE
FOUNDATION

WHAT DOES IT MEAN
TO BE A LATINO?

This chapter discusses what it means to be Latino: the assimilation process; your language; strong relationships; networks; and, how to take advantage of the diversity trend in America. Before you begin reading, however, we would like for you to take a minute to reflect on and answer the following questions.

- How well do you know your heritage? (Do you know the stories of those who emigrated before you, where they come from, what they went through, and so on?)
- Could you describe what traits or skills made your family or yourself (if you are the first generation in this country) successful in the U.S. or in your country of origin?
- How are you taking advantage of those skills?
- If it applies, how are you teaching those skills to your children?

The answers to these questions are quite important, because the only way to make the most out of your innate skills and traits is to know what you are made of and where you originally came from. It is about going back to your roots.

If you are lucky and your family has done a good job keeping history alive, you certainly have vivid role models and success stories (or stories of failure) that show you alternative ways of approaching problems. We will help you connect with that knowledge and then use it in a productive way.

THE BATTLE TO BELONG

Whether it was your grandparents, your parents, or you personally who first came to the U.S., starting again in a new country—with a different language, culture, and customs—is not an easy undertaking. There are different strategies to overcome the obstacles presented during immigration. For many generations, most immigrants (Latinos included) found that the best way to overcome these obstacles was to do whatever it took in order to fit in to the new system, even at the expense of forgetting everything connected to their past. The other extreme, also followed by many immigrants, was to recreate their original country in the new country, to live in the past as if nothing had changed.

Pure observation would show that couples with young children might go for the first strategy (focusing on their kids mainly), while many older people choose the other extreme (focusing on themselves). This is, of course, a generalization, and you will find immigrants of all conditions, ages, and origins in both these groups, but it seems that these are the more common strategies in the battle to assimilate to the new culture.

This book, however, strives to show you an alternative strategy, a more balanced approach to assimilation that tries to incorporate the best from your original culture while also incorporating positive elements of your new society. The examples in this chapter show three different ways of dealing with this process of blending into the new society. They are not the only ways, but they will give you some ideas of how people cope with this issue.

EXAMPLE

Haydee was born in the U.S. to Puerto Rican parents who did not speak Spanish to Haydee as she was growing up. They were determined to help her become an American quickly and not be singled out as the *Latina girl* in school. Now she works at a bank in an area highly populated by Latinos, who approach her speaking Spanish the moment they see her name plate. She feels embarrassed every time she has to confess that she speaks only English. A few months ago, she took it upon herself to sign up for Spanish classes at a community college.

Haydee's situation is still very common, and admittedly this strategy has some positive effects. To become an American, one does need to learn the new rules of the game, so that is what Haydee's parents did. However, their daughter is now suffering some of the downsides of their early efforts to fit in into the system. In a country where Latinos are the fastest growing minority and where all the statistics show that they are becoming a dominant force in America's economy, being able to speak the language of all these consumers is an advantage. Being a professional with this skill is a valuable asset to any kind of business, whether a big corporation or a small neighborhood store.

Alternatively, many people do not feel comfortable trying to learn all these new rules and customs; therefore, they work to counter this incredibly strong force by recreating their home country within their host country. These are the people who refuse to give up any of their original customs and show no interest in learning anything about the American system. They never learn the language or eat anything but food from the old country.

EXAMPLE

Ernestina is a Mexican journalist who came to the U.S. to follow her partner. She left her family and a good job back home to be here with him. She did not have the drive to learn English or anything related to the U.S. She turned her house into a Mexican shrine—celebrating all her traditions and speaking on the phone only with

> her family. She did not try to get a job here or make any
> friends. It was not long before she realized that she was
> not happy. She could not relate to anything around her
> and she began to feel lonely and homesick. She went
> back and forth between the U.S. and Mexico until she
> finally decided to look for a job as a journalist in the
> States. Although she found it difficult to get around
> given her language limitations, she did get a position
> where she was assigned an interpreter to interview
> American politicians for a Latino newspaper.

In Ernestina's case, her initial rejection of anything American isolated her and made her understandably unhappy. She was not able to fully integrate and progress in any area of her life, including the professional one. Once she was able to apply her professional training in an environment where she could take advantage of her culture, she began to integrate both worlds.

MAXIMIZING OPPORTUNITIES

As you move forward, keep in mind that your goal is to maximize the possibilities of the American system by bringing forward your diverse cultural heritage. A diverse heritage means that you have more ingredients in your talent mix. You learned a different set of rules, multiple ways to look at the world, and different ways to relate to and work with people. All this makes you a richer person at a time when the U.S. labor market needs a diversity of ideas and solutions to continue growing and developing. This is a case of *more is more*—having two cultures is better than having only one. Therein lies the Latino advantage.

It should be pointed out that the idea of cultural diversity as an asset was not always popular in America. As much as this country is described as a *melting pot*, concerns over losing the "true" American identity are raised every now and then. The way this book approaches this debate is to help you bring out the best that you have inside in order to maximize your career success. It is all about gaining an edge that will help you differentiate and compete more effectively in the modern economy.

A Word about the Exercises

The objective of these activities is to help you reflect upon your origins and some of the advantages (and disadvantages) you already have as a result of your heritage. Many of these are things you do without thinking much—ways of approaching an issue, resolving a problem, interacting with people, and so on. Analyzing them and breaking them down into smaller pieces will help you understand what you are doing and how you are doing it. It will be a bit hard at first, but after a few activities, you will be able to extract the generic skills that your Latino upbringing has given you and apply them to different settings.

LET'S PRACTICE

To increase your awareness regarding the impact of your cultural background in your workplace, start with a simple activity.

■ List a few instances when your Latino background helped you in any way (e.g., someone shared important information with you, you got a better assignment at work, etc.).

_____

_____

_____

■ Why do you think this happened?

_____

_____

_____

Now think of the opposite situation.

■ List a few instances when your Latino background hindered your progress at work in any way (e.g., people made assumptions about your behavior or your abilities, etc.).

_____

_____

_____

■ Why do you think this happened? (Try to think of things you actively did. If you were the object of a discriminatory action, reflect on that as well.)

_____

_____

_____

USING YOUR LANGUAGE

Language is one of the most powerful ways to build relationships and create connections. Imagine if you spoke several languages. Wouldn't that give you an advantage over others with fewer abilities? It seems like an obvious answer, and yet, how many fellow Latinos do you know who have forgotten their heritage language? What about you—have you let one of your big advantages slip away?

Considering the projected growth in both new immigration and births to Latino parents, there will be more and more opportunities in the U.S. for those with multiple language abilities. However, the most important point is that there are millions of people out there with

CAREER TIP

You should always add your language skills to your résumé. Many people just do so if they think that it is applicable to the job they are applying for, but the reality is that you never know how things can evolve. Having an additional language (even if your knowledge of it is rather basic) is a very important asset in the modern world. Always let others know about all the skills you have.

whom you have an immediate point of connection. You know the password that will make you part of their club (and vice versa), because these are people with whom you share traditions, taste, values, and so on. These are people who will go the extra mile to help you out, and they are the first group you should tap into as you learn more about your Latino advantage.

LET'S PRACTICE

If you have not experienced language as a tool to establish relationships yet, try any of the following. Write about what happens in each situation on the lines provided.

- At a restaurant, when you notice that the waiter or the host speaks Spanish, order in Spanish. If you cannot, at least say "Hola, ¿cómo está?" If you are the waiter and you notice that a guest speaks Spanish, welcome him or her in that language.

_____

_____

_____

- At your child's school, when you notice that an administrative person speaks Spanish, talk to him or her in Spanish.

_____

_____

_____

- If you meet someone you like and he or she has a Latino background, say a few words in Spanish and observe the reaction.

_____

_____

_____

When you use your language skills even in these casual ways, you will see a spark in the eyes of those you talk to, and you most likely will feel a connection that will translate into better service, a bigger tip, and all kinds of opportunities.

Remember, building relationships and networking require a starting point. An additional language can (and will) give you an additional advantage—you will have another way of making that initial connection with the forty-one million Latinos in the U.S. Showing that you have something in common will help you overcome the initial mistrust that has become customary in the modern world. Show your fellow Latinos that you are one of them—that somewhere there are points of connection with them. This will give you an advantage.

EXAMPLE

In his role as human resources manager, Carlos coaches both employees and managers through many conflicts in the workplace. Once, during an exit interview (a meeting an employer has with an employee who decides to leave the company), Hernán, a Latino employee, was telling Carlos about his decision-making process in leaving. At a critical point in the conversation he switched from English to Spanish. Carlos knew what this meant—Hernán was sharing with him sensitive information. Hernán knew that all the information Carlos handled as an HR manager was confidential in nature, but this was his way of letting Carlos know that this issue was particularly sensitive and it required extra care. They both benefited. Hernán was able to tell Carlos more than he would have had Carlos not been Latino, and Carlos gathered additional information about the environment in the office that could help him improve the climate in the company.

This was pure Latino advantage at play for both sides. Using Spanish with your fellow Latinos can make people feel comfortable with you and give you more information, better service, and opportunities that they would not have, had you not spoken the language.

UNIFORMITY VS. DIVERSITY

Think about how products compete against each other—usually by adding a feature that other products in the market do not have. The market, however, is quite efficient in this process, and when you see a cell phone that has a camera, for example, within months all cell phones have cameras. Whenever a company finds a new feature that is more costly or difficult to copy, it obtains a higher than average return for a longer period of time. This higher return is maintained until the competition catches up. This process is repeated over and over again regardless of the industry.

One thing is for sure—in today's highly competitive economic system, success is mainly about differentiation. This was not the norm many years ago, when uniformity was the rule. Think back to when the only car available was a black Model T Ford, or when everybody had a black telephone. In order to achieve profitability, companies counted on volume and marketed the same product to everyone. Market segmentation was an untapped concept.

Nowadays, if you do not target your product to almost each individual, you do not stand a chance. Think about the ring tones you can choose to customize your cell phone, or cars like the Mini Cooper that you can design on the dealer's computer according to your specifications.

Consider that the same dynamic that goes on with consumer products applies to people. How do you distinguish (or differentiate) yourself from others as a person and as a professional? How do you customize yourself so you stand out from the crowd? Usually, you learn new skills, take additional training, and get a college degree.

However, as time goes by, it is getting much more difficult to stand out, and those additional skills are easily learned by others. Twenty years ago, having a college degree gave you an absolute edge; today, it just helps you catch up with the rest. Besides, despite how much more comfortable and easier technology has made our lives, it has also made getting a competitive edge a lot more complicated. Since most information is available to everyone through the different technology-enabled media (especially the Internet), every day there are fewer competitive advantages that can give you the edge you need in the race to success. This process will only accelerate as time goes by.

This is where the Latino advantage comes into play. You have an edge inside yourself. The beauty of this is that your advantage, your new feature, cannot be easily copied by others.

CAREER TIP

Use diversity to your advantage. There are many companies making extraordinary efforts to ensure they have a diverse workforce, and there are multiple associations that are working hard to bring Latinos together. Refer to the resources section to learn more about diversity job boards and professional Latino associations. (see Appendix A.)

You do not need to look far to find the edge that will help you stand out—diversity, one of the key strengths in today's economic world, is already part of who you are. Also, remember that it does not matter how hidden your Latino roots are—they are always part of who you are.

2

THE
BALANCING ACT

While your Latino traits provide you with numerous advantages, there are stereotypes and behaviors tied to our heritage that are counterproductive in the American system. These are things that may be quite normal in your heritage country but still create an uncomfortable reaction from other Americans in the U.S. The following is an example that illustrates how not paying attention to cultural differences could have a negative impact on success.

EXAMPLE

Marisol is a receptionist at a large and busy dental office. She is very friendly and is proud of her Latino roots, which contribute to her extreme sociability. Most of the time she speaks loudly on the phone, and unfortunately, because she is so friendly, her supervisors do not know if she is talking to a patient or making a personal call.

One day, she got a call from her daughter's school. Apparently, her child was being sent home for the third time that week because she was sick. Marisol became increasingly loud until she began to yell at the person at the other end. The reception area was full of patients, and other employees witnessed Marisol falling apart. Following this incident, Marisol was sent to special customer service training. When asked about what she thought her problem was, she said that her supervisor did not like her being nice and sociable with patients. In fact, this trait was very much appreciated by her bosses, as it helped patients who were normally under a lot of stress relax.

Marisol was completely unaware that her problem came from setting no boundaries between personal and business matters. Her private life was public, and that was not good for business. In America, there is a tendency to separate personal and business matters more strictly than in other places. In this case, Marisol's Latino trait crossed the line and turned into a disadvantage in this environment.

STEREOTYPES AND THE BATTLE FOR BALANCE

Finding the right balance between fitting into the new system and actually assimilating (that is, adopting the new system as your own while using your innate differences to succeed) is not an easy task. Many Latinos are too self-conscious about existing stereotypes and do their best to avoid being associated with them. It will not be easy to identify a particular trait that causes negative reactions or to overcome it, as some of our behaviors are very ingrained. Still, the rewards for succeeding are absolutely worth the effort.

You should always remember that there is an abundance of stereotypes about Latinos, and those stereotypes have been built based on observed behaviors. The challenge of stereotypes is that those perceptions are a reality to those who have them. Therefore, people tend to act, even preemptively, based on them. Refer to the examples regarding *Latino time* discussed on page xvii. In those situations, people acted as if the stereotype of Latinos and their time management applied to everyone and in every situation.

As if this were not enough of a challenge, you have to be aware that a minor slip on your behalf will only reinforce the stereotypes. While being late to a meeting, lunch date, or event can happen to anyone, if you are a Latino, it will most likely be used to "confirm" the general perception.

For all these reasons, many of you have made efforts to distance yourselves from those perceptions and stereotypes, and therefore will react with some skepticism to some of the advantages of embracing your Latino traits. Just keep in mind that it is all about finding the right balance. After all, you cannot control other people's behaviors— you can only control your own.

LET'S PRACTICE

List a situation in which you made a big effort to move away from your own Latino heritage (it could be to avoid a stereotype). For example, you may have denied your origin by not telling anyone at work that you could speak or understand Spanish, decided not to join a Hispanic network in your company, or made negative comments about Latinos to your colleagues to make sure nobody would associate you with them.

■ What was the situation?

_____

_____

_____

_____

_____

■ What did you do?

_____

_____

■ What was the stereotype (lateness, unreliability, etc.)?

_____

_____

■ What was the explanation you gave yourself as a justification for your actions?

_____

_____

■ What was the outcome?

_____

_____

Now, try to think of the same situation and consider ways in which you could embrace your culture, maximize the advantages it can bring to the workplace, and still be part of the American culture.

■ What would you do differently?

_____

_____

_____

■ What edge would that approach give you?

_____

_____

_____

■ How can you turn the situation around now? (For example, if in the past you decided not to join the Hispanic network in the office, you can join it now.)

_____

_____

EXAMPLE

Marion's parents immigrated to the U.S. before she was born, and other than Spanish spoken at home, English was her language. Influenced by her parents, Marion made many efforts to fit in the American system and leave behind any traces of her Latino roots, which meant that, if not for her last name, nobody could have guessed she was Latina. Working for a large multinational company, she climbed up the ladder mainly due to her strong accounting skills and her ability to work extremely well with difficult clients. Although there was a Hispanic network in the company, she never joined because she had made it a big point not to be considered different from her colleagues in any way, and because she had not told anyone that she could speak Spanish fluently.

A couple of years ago, the company she was working for acquired a large financial services institution in Mexico. The project had a lot of visibility, and there was a strong need for skilled professionals who could not only speak the language, but also understand the Latino way of doing business.

Marion had made such an effort to deny any connection to her Latino roots that she could not figure out a way to disclose her skills. She felt people would think that she had been hiding something.

Marion ultimately decided not to say anything, and the company ended up hiring someone from the outside to be part of the integration team. Because of this, Marion missed multiple opportunities to use her advantage without losing any of her American status.

If Marion had realized that having a Latino background was nothing to be ashamed of, and understood how to turn her diverse cultural background to her advantage (additional language, experience with different perspectives, etc.), her career would have taken a huge turn for the better. She could have developed a network of contacts within her company who were aware not only of her heritage, but of her skills and talents, and who would have considered her at the time of the promotion.

The important lesson about this example is that you will only be really successful (and happy) if you are in control of your career and your life. There is absolutely nothing wrong with disclosing less information in order to avoid being labeled. Many professionals, upon deciding on a different course for their career, will not talk much about what they did before. The key, however, is that you have to be in the driver's seat and make the decisions.

CAREER TIP

If you are in the middle of a career change or if you do not want to be labeled in a particular way, an effective method to signal your career plans is including a profile or career objective at the beginning of your résumé. This gives your potential interviewer a key to read your background and understand where you want to go without you having to exclude any substantial experience from the résumé.

Be careful that in your quest to fit in into the American culture you do not deny your origins. When you do, you lose your strengths, and that is what makes you unique in your approach to life. There is a saying that you should always keep in mind—*the longer the roots, the stronger the tree.* Your roots are important and made you who you are. However, they do not define you completely. You define yourself through every decision that you make.

PROFILE
Ana Duarte-McCarthy—Chief Player

Considering that Ana Duarte-McCarthy is the Chief Diversity Officer at one of the largest companies in the world, you would expect a high-wired woman. Yet, when you meet her, you are immediately taken by her friendly and peaceful demeanor. She has achieved a wonderful balance between cultures and languages in her career.

Ana was born in the U.S. to Dominican parents who came to this country in order for her father to do his medical residency. "They never intended to come and stay, so suddenly my mother, who like a lot of other people had a comfortable life back home, had to work at a factory to help support the family," Ana shares.

She grew up between Chicago and New Jersey. She spoke Spanish and English at home and mostly English outside the home, since at the time there were few Spanish-speaking neighbors in areas that later became large Latino enclaves.

With a graduate degree in Counseling and Organizational Psychology, Ana Duarte-McCarthy spent the first ten to twelve years of her career working in higher education, first providing counseling services and then as the Director of Counseling and Opportunities at the New School for Social Research. She then migrated to the private sector to work on diversity, a new area that was just opening up, and in 1995 she joined Citibank. "I felt it was important to do this kind of work with a company that had a global orientation," she explains.

Ana believes that speaking Spanish has given her a great advantage in her career, as it has always enabled her to become a key person at her different jobs, given that she could communicate in this language with all levels of the administration and clients.

Leveraging her language skills and her Latino background was perfect to pursue a career in the diversity field. "People need to study English," she stresses while reflecting on how many Latinos remain within their own community without learning the language and also without getting an education. "Latinos also need to find out about the great number of partnership opportunities that are out there to help them get an education or find a job." For example, when you are looking to work for a new company, Ana suggests that you find out if they have any Latino networks or mentoring programs where you can have colleagues teach you the corporate culture—the unwritten rules of the company. "Find out if this is a company that will embrace your culture or will want you to be a specific type of employee within a certain corporate culture," she recommends.

Of course, just like everybody else, Ana has encountered obstacles in her career because of her cultural background. At times she felt like she was being placed on all sorts of committees only because she was Latina. At other times she felt people were condescending towards her. The one thing she always did, however, was evaluate how much of what was happening was a result of her own conditioning and how much it was something else.

"Minority people always carry the potential that an experience is biased. So, if somebody cuts in front of you at the grocery store, are they doing it because they are rude? Are they doing it because you are a woman? Is it because you are Latino? All these questions might go through your head. If you were a white male you pretty much think it's because the person is rude." Ana says that minorities many times walk through life wondering if the events in their life and interactions with other people are connected to their ethnicity. She suggests that the more you manage that thinking pattern, the better, because it is a heavy weight to carry around. "The key," she points out, "is to see if those obstacles are perceived or real, recognize racism when it's there, and don't let it limit you."

Whenever the circumstances point at a biased or discriminatory situation, Ana is the first one to confront it in a way that is productive—maybe taking aside the person who has made a comment and talking privately. Not speaking up is definitely not the way to go.

Another area in which Ana strongly believes people should get involved is education. "The fight now is for talent. The pool of diversity talent is not keeping pace with the demand." Her conviction that education is the way to a brighter future is easily put into perspective when you hear her say that "the Baby Boom generation is aging and leaving the workforce at an alarming rate. We don't have a replacement population ready. That presents an enormous opportunity for Latinos to replace those workers, because we are the growing minority in the country." Getting the best possible education and learning English fluently is really the way to achieve success.

More and more companies value employees from different cultures who know how to work in other countries and who can work cross-culturally. "The truth is," Ana says, "that a lot of people whose families have been here for several generations envy people with strong cultural values because they don't have cultural values themselves and they feel lost sometimes."

Ana Duarte-McCarthy has always been on the cutting edge of what is going on in the diversity field in this country. Her advice is crucial for anyone trying to move on with his or her career in a competitive market. Whether you work at a small company or at a large corporation, whether you just finished college or are looking to change jobs, you should take advantage of her insights regarding how Latinos can be the *replacement generation*. With a close focus on your education and language fluency, you can turn these insights into gold.

∾

PART 2

THE LATINO
ADVANTAGES

3

VALUES

The rule of law and the importance of individual rights have always been a key component of the American system, much more so than in any other country. Since the September 11th attacks, the discussions around values have become increasingly important in American life. These days, Americans are focused mainly on values that revolve around personal responsibility, the importance of family, and the role of spirituality and religion in everyday life. What is quite interesting is that some of these ideas being valued in America today are those that Latinos have long held, and they used to make it harder for Latinos to connect to this culture.

When it comes to values, Latinos have always been perceived as very conservative, family-oriented, and mostly followers of the Catholic church, something that years ago created some dissonance with the mainstream culture in America, where Protestantism is the most widespread religion. In recent years, as America united against extreme fundamentalist movements that produced terrorist attacks, moderate Christian values (including Catholic) got a big boost in popularity and acceptance. Strong family ties, spirituality, and religion have become more important in America. As a matter of fact, Latino values are now closer to mainstream values than ever before, giving us a great opportunity for integration.

Not everyone sees it this way, however. If you follow any of the discussions surrounding immigration, you will notice that the groups opposing it are concerned that the different values of the immigrating cultures will make America lose its identity. That is definitely not the case with Latinos. Latino values and American values are more in sync today than they have ever been. As a Latino, you have to be aware of your real similarities with the American culture. This realization will help you move away from the temptation to forget what your heritage is and who you are in order to fit in.

There are many, many values in a culture and it would be nearly impossible to talk about all of them. However, there are certain key values common in most Latinos that, when incorporated into your work life, can give you a big advantage.

THE IMPORTANCE OF FAMILY

Chapter 4 talks more in-depth about how the absence of a strong and steady rule of law in Latin American countries made personal relationships and the immediate network essential for survival. Family became the foundation of this immediate network that Latinos hold so dear.

In fact, it is interesting to compare the Latino and the American family side by side. Latinos are always surprised by how detached the members of an American family seem to be. Even though there is a lot of focus on parenting during the early years, the connection loosens as children grow up, usually until the point when the family only comes together for the holidays. (A clear example of this is the fact that at eighteen, many American children leave home to go to college—something seldom done in Latin American countries.)

CAREER TIP

It is acceptable, during interviews, to express how important your family and your values are to you. It is also okay to talk about the role models who inspired you and influence who you are today. It is an effective way to make a positive connection with the person interviewing you.

In general, Latinos do not feel very comfortable with this detached approach to family life. In a Latino household, it is not uncommon to have multiple generations living under the same roof, with authority figures still being very influential at later stages in life. What you need to do at this point is to make the connection between who you are when you are at home and how those traits could give you an edge outside your home.

LET'S PRACTICE

Think about an important party that you organized for your family. It can be a quinceañera or a wedding—it does not matter. Try to recall all the people you invited, plus the people you talked to in order to make it happen. You probably spoke to lots of individuals you know well to help you coordinate the food, music, decorations, clothing, location, and so on.

■ Make a list of all the activities that were involved.

_____

_____

■ List any obstacles you had to overcome during the organization of this event (for example, having to invite members of the family that do not particularly get along and decide how to sit them) and how you worked with your network to overcome those obstacles.

_____

_____

Now think for a moment about your job. Pretend that you have to organize an event (a conference or a party for other employees or for customers). Do you have the contacts you need to pull off a successful event? The skills you need to produce a successful event at work are the same you use at home to pull off a successful party.

> ■ Do you notice that sometimes when it comes to establishing relationships you behave differently at work than at home? (For instance, you are shy to approach new people.) What are some of those differences?
>
> _____
>
> _____

The truth is that you learned from early on how to establish strong and long-lasting relationships with your family and close friends. That is why it is probably not that easy for you to venture beyond that tight circle.

LOYALTY

The topic of loyalty is closely related to the importance of family teachings in the Latino culture. Latinos are usually recognized for being very loyal, especially to family and close friends. Loyalty is a valuable asset in the modern world, and it is critical when it comes to work and professional relationships.

The idea of loyalty feeds a number of other traits, such as the ability to forge strong and productive networks. It is easy to see that without some degree of loyalty, it is impossible to develop the strong relationships needed to establish strong networks.

There are shortcomings associated with this behavior when taken to the extreme. Consider those situations in which the informal rules created by networks and relationships conflict with the rule of law. In many Latin American countries, you learn that when this happens, you first need to protect relationships, as more often than not they are longer lasting than the law or rule being enforced at

CAREER TIP

In an interview, be prepared to show specific examples that illustrate positive traits like loyalty, and show the value to your prospective employer. Try to pick those that are more related to a work environment, but personal ones are acceptable too.

the time. In America, when the law is involved there are no considerations to make—you just respect it. This behavior gives Latinos somewhat of a mixed reputation, as we are perceived as too ready to protect friends and family even in extreme situations.

You have been raised to be loyal to friends and family, and you know what is owed to others. This is a key trait to apply beyond your close-knit network, and use it at work to advance your career. For example, your loyalty to your company will enable you to protect company secrets, and loyalty to a coworker will make it easier to back him or her up when he or she has a new idea to present to the boss. However, if not applied properly, this trait can work to your disadvantage. For example, you should never allow your loyalty to your coworkers or your boss to cloud your judgment if they are engaged in insider trading or other illegal activities. Keep your shortcomings in check, and beware of choosing friends and family above the rule of law.

HONESTY

Few people would argue against the idea that Latinos are raised in a disciplined and conservative family environment. The idea of doing the right thing has been instilled in every Latino from the beginning of his or her life. However, it is also true that if pushed to choose between doing the right thing as per the rules or doing the right thing as per personal (and communal) feelings, most Latinos would choose the second option. This is very different from typical American values. America is a country of laws—probably one of the most legalistic countries there is. Americans value the rule of law above personal relationships.

It is inaccurate to say that Latinos do not respect the law. In fact, Latinos are well recognized for being law-abiding citizens who collaborate with authorities whenever they can. It is only when forced to choose between family values and societal values (rules and laws) that Latinos tend to favor family ones.

For this reason, it is relevant for you to spend some time reflecting about this topic. It is essential to understand the impact of your actions and the image that you are passing on those around you. Keep in mind that perception is reality for those who have that perception, and your success will greatly depend on how well you manage your image.

LET'S PRACTICE

Write down a situation in which your internal values conflicted with a particular rule or law and how you dealt with the situation. The goal of this exercise is to reflect on the good intentions you might have had (or will have in the future) in instances such as this one, and the impact of your actions. There will be plenty of gray areas in which the right answer will be difficult to find, but it is critical to understand how people with different values and cultural backgrounds would perceive these actions.

Use the following example as a guide.
- Situation: My coworker is stealing expensive office supplies.
- Your action: I do not report her.
- Your perspective: I privilege our friendship over a rule.
- Alternate perspective: These supplies are for the office, so it hurts me too to have them stolen. I'll report her to the boss.
- Impact of your action: I'm reinforcing my friend's wrong behavior and hurting the office as a whole.
- Other possible reactions and effects: I talk to my coworker to explain the impact of her behavior and warn her that this is the last time I will keep quiet.

- Situation:
_____
_____

■ Your action:

_____

_____

■ Your perspective:

_____

_____

■ Alternate perspective:

_____

_____

■ Impact of your action:

_____

_____

■ Other possible reactions and effects:

_____

_____

Remember, what the world sees is not the intention of your actions, but their impact. Think about what your intention was when you behaved that way. Think about what the impact of your behavior was. Finally, try to put yourself in an American's shoes and think about how they would have reacted in the same situation.

You know what is right. You have been brought up with excellent values. Honesty between friends and family is a value you grew up with. Having a reputation at work as being an honest person will earn you respect, and ultimately, advancement. But again, always be diligent about keeping your shortcomings in check. Understand the impact of siding with your personal relationships and sacrificing rules and laws that are there to regulate and protect everybody's relationships with each other. Understand how the perception people have of you can have a real impact on your life. Being perceived as someone who cannot clearly see the difference between loyalty and honesty will drastically limit your opportunities to advance in your career and in life in general in this country.

GOAL SETTING

The history of all immigrant groups has a lot in common, especially when it comes to hard work and sacrifice. All these groups left a lot behind in order to start a new life in America. Starting a new life is a very challenging undertaking. You have to learn a new language and new rules. There is clearly a lot of sacrifice and a lot of work involved, and goal setting is often an important part of the undertaking.

LET'S PRACTICE

Think about the first generation of your family that came to America—those special people who broke new ground or achieved new objectives. Try to visualize them. Put yourself in their shoes. If you are not that familiar with the details, do some research on it. If you are that person, then you will have to go back to your own thoughts and objectives when you started planning to come over to America.

The objective of this exercise is to reconstruct a success story. Yes, leaving your home country and starting a new life is in itself a success story. You set a goal and you achieved it. In all likelihood, when you look into your family's history (or into your own), you will find that the key to success is to structure your efforts in an efficient way.

Once you have your family story, answer the following questions.

■ What were the goals they/you set out to achieve?

_____

_____

_____

- How did they/you go about organizing themselves/yourself to achieve those goals?

  _____

  _____

  _____

- What short-term sacrifices did they/you make in order to obtain longer-term goals?

  _____

  _____

  _____

- Set out a chronology of events.

  _____

  _____

  _____

- Consider other questions you think may be valuable to ask. (For example, how did they advance in their careers? Did they find mentors along the way?)

  _____

  _____

  _____

Use this exercise as a practice on how to set small goals for yourself and on how to organize your actions towards those goals.

The Latino advantage lies, once again, in looking back into your history and finding out how others succeeded before you and how they reached their goals. You can gain great inspiration from their stories and even from your own beginnings (if you were the first one to come to the U.S.).

EXAMPLE

Vicente had just received his finance degree when he arrived in the U.S. speaking no English. For the first three years, he cleaned houses while he studied English at night. Every time he interviewed with a prospective client, he offered to clean the house every other week. He figured that way he could charge more and have more clients, which would give him more stability on the job. Within two months he was cleaning two houses a day and had a waiting list.

You or your family set an incredibly difficult goal that you already achieved—coming to America. You understand that in order to achieve a goal, you will need to make some sacrifices and work hard. You have multiple role models to inspire you. Latinos are more comfortable setting broad goals, the kind that can be modified easily and changed frequently. Americans, on the other hand, learn from a very early age to plan extremely detailed and specific objectives. The stability of the environment encourages this behavior. Now that you are here in America, remember to set small, achievable goals that you can stick to and that will lead you to your long-term goals.

CAREER TIP

When prospective employers interview you, they are expecting organized and well thought-out career plans that have been executed according to a schedule. They also like to see that decisions have been made rationally and can be explained. It is very important that you train yourself to tell your story this way. State your objectives clearly and make sure you can explain your work and career decisions. It is good to show adaptability to a changing environment, but complete improvisation and emotional or erratic decision making does not project a positive image.

RESPECT FOR AUTHORITY

The relationship of Latinos with authority is quite complex. For those who immigrated to the U.S. as young adults and adults, their heritage countries continue to exert a strong influence. This means that often two different sets of rules develop—how things work in America, and how things work in Latin American countries. Even if you do not know much about the history of your family, you surely know that the freedoms enjoyed in America are not always present in other parts of the world. In Latin America in particular, there is a history of dictatorships and paternalistic democracies that have molded our view of the world. When you add to this dimension the importance of authority figures in a typical Latin American family, you can develop a clearer picture of how our relationship with authority was built.

Latinos have a good reputation for working well in hierarchical structures. They respect authority, generally have a low confrontational style, and are good at following direction and getting things done. Latinos typically possess a great deal of flexibility, and that trait makes them good team players. Latinos are also well known for their work ethic. One of the reasons why this group has become so successful in America is directly linked to this ability. In a big and complex production machine like America, employers are always in need of resources to keep it moving, and Latinos have become an essential and sought after component.

EXAMPLE

Ray, originally from Ecuador, migrated to the U.S. in the early nineties. Back home, he was mainly a carpenter, but he also took some jobs painting houses and in construction. He came to the U.S. in response to the strong demand for qualified construction workers. Since he arrived, he has been working for a small construction company. Ray not only has gained an excellent reputation for the quality of his work, but also for how reliable and easygoing he is. He takes direction quite well, and is respectful with the contractors, architects, and clients. For Ray, these traits have always come naturally, but he has realized that in general that is not the case in his line of work. He has also started to notice that he is getting more and better jobs because of his good manners and respect for authority.

However, that same respect for authority can be carried too far and become submission. Clearly this is not the desired trait for anyone in America, where individual rights are held in high regard. Additionally, being too submissive to authority subtracts much of the value that Latinos bring to the table. It is not that difficult to express your opinions, and even disagree, in a respectful manner. Remember that a diversity of opinions enriches an organization, as they provide it with alternative solutions to problems and creative ways of approaching old ideas.

EXAMPLE

Jason is a paralegal in a medium-sized law firm in New York. Everyone values the quality of his contributions and how hard he works. They also know that he is pursuing his law degree at night so he is more knowledgeable than the average paralegal in the group. Jason, however, is not that happy. He feels that he could be contributing more (especially now that he is closer to obtaining his degree), but he finds it extremely difficult to express his opinions. Often, working with some of the less experienced lawyers, he sees the mistakes they make and the critical points they miss while dealing with clients, but he cannot bring himself to point them out. In his mind, it would be inappropriate for him to point out their mistakes because they are lawyers and he is not.

Taking a closer look at Jason's background helps explain this trepidation. He was born in the U.S. to Mexican parents who immigrated in the sixties. Although they all consider themselves completely American, their family interactions are still very much guided by their old traditions. Jason's father is a strong authority figure, and Jason learned early on the importance of hierarchy and how roles should be respected. Even though Jason knows that things are quite different in America, he still cannot find the right way to approach these situations.

You may have felt like Jason at one point or another. There are times when you probably notice that something you were taught while growing up does not quite apply to the world that you live in. Keep in mind that regardless of where you come from, your upbringing has a strong influence on you, and working around them takes time, effort, and practice.

LET'S PRACTICE

Think of a situation where your upbringing conflicted with the way things are done in America. For example, you may address your boss more formally or greet people at a company party by kissing them on the cheek, like many Latinos are used to. Now think about how these same things are done here and consider the critical difference. How does that difference impact you?

Being overly formal might delay creating a productive relationship with your boss or make you feel less comfortable to express your ideas with him or her. At the company party, touching others when you talk, or kissing them, might make people uncomfortable or feel that you are invading their space.

- How would you approach these different situations now? List your strategies and action plan.

_____

_____

_____

_____

_____

KNOW YOURSELF

Respect for authority is indeed a difficult topic to cover. This is not to say that Latinos cannot function well in a democratic environment, or that privileging the authority of the father in the family is not an appropriate value. Rather, the traditions that are part of your heritage offer you experiences, both good and bad, that can make you stronger and more effective in a different society, like the American one.

The fact that you respect authority makes you a great employee because you can follow direction well without feeling the need to question motives excessively. When given a task, you can usually get down to business right away.

In the following example, you will see that since you are used to the importance authority has in any organized structure, you have become very creative and resourceful when it comes to challenging the status quo. Emilio's story is a clear example of resourceful problem solving and how to deal with authority in a creative and positive way. In addition, you will also see in this example how your cooperative nature, added to your respect for authority, makes you a wonderful team player in the workforce.

CAREER TIP

Planning and crafting your message carefully is essential when you are proposing a new strategy. Do not get frustrated if it takes several tries before you can make others see things from your perspective. Also, regardless of how hierarchical your place of work is, as long as you are respectful and have a well laid-out plan of what you are asking for or proposing, you should not get into trouble.

EXAMPLE

In the news industry, companies are rarely able to expand in the fourth quarter because that is the time of the year when advertising dollars are running out. However, Emilio, the new news director at the local station of a major Hispanic broadcasting company, wanted to expand to end his first year at the job on a positive note. He knew he would get into trouble, since his bosses might think that he did not understand the business, unless he could pull off his plan in an innovative way. He created five new five-minute segments that would offer local city weather and traffic information within the national morning news programming. Emilio then found one advertiser per segment to cover his cost and had two additional advertisers on a waiting list. He could now begin in the black, with no start-up costs or losses. Knowing how to maximize scarce resources—something a lot of Latinos learned in their countries of origin—is a good skill to put into practice at work, one that allowed Emilio to disagree with the way things had always been done while offering a way to support his position.

Your relationship with authority has a positive impact at work. You follow direction well and you are a good team player. However, always remember that your experience with authoritarian figures may have triggered a tendency to submission. This is a trait you should observe closely, as it is not valued in America.

THE NEED TO PLEASE

Being loyal and able to work efficiently in a hierarchical environment require reliability as a key value in the mix. However, you are probably familiar with the stereotype that Latinos are not very reliable. The reason is that on some occasions, certain aspects of our culture may contribute to building a bad reputation.

Consider the following idea. Generally speaking, Latinos do not feel comfortable confronting others (much less when that person is the boss). Latinos would much rather find ways of pleasing people than disappointing them. This is one of the reasons why Latinos succeed in jobs that involve customer relations. That is why often, even when it is known from the beginning that it will be very difficult to please a customer or a boss, Latinos delay giving the bad news until it is probably too late. The following examples illustrate this point.

EXAMPLE

When Richard called his housecleaner, Analía, and asked her if she was available to clean his apartment on Saturday morning before a lunch he was hosting, Analía said she could be there at 10 a.m. At 11 a.m., she had not arrived or called and Richard was getting rather impatient, as his guests would be arriving at 12:30. He began cleaning himself and was in the middle of it when Analía arrived at 11:45. Analía explained that she had two other customers on Saturday, but she had wanted to help Richard as well. This would have been a good time for Analía to have said no to Richard's request. It would have given him the opportunity to make alternative arrangements. Analía thought she was providing excellent service by making herself available to her customers, but she missed the impact of her behavior. Now, not only had she not helped Richard, but she had made him so angry that she would probably lose him as a customer.

This rather simple example may make it seem like some occupations have a higher concentration of "unreliable" people. Nonetheless, in general terms, occupations that require direct contact with customers and where there is a lot of perceived distance between boss and employee, saying no is somewhat more difficult.

EXAMPLE

Lisa has agreed to her friend Mario's request to try his printing company. She works at a nonprofit organization that prints lots of fliers and brochures, and Mario has been asking her to give him a try for a long time. Lisa needed 1,000 invitations printed a week from Friday, so she decided to ask Mario to print them for her. Mario took the job, reassuring Lisa that he would have it ready on time, but knowing that he was backed up with prior jobs that were also urgent. He could not finish Lisa's job on time. He did not let her know in advance, and she missed her deadline.

This behavior is probably one of the more difficult to change. Latinos in general do not like conflict and want to please people, sometimes by telling them what they want to hear. While this makes Latinos very nice people to be around and probably contributes to their success in America, keep in mind that in this country, reliability is a stronger value than being nice. If you are perceived as nice but are known to be unreliable, you will not go as far in your career as you could. By learning to set expectations beforehand and eventually learning to say no in a way that does not conflict with your natural style, you can gain an important edge.

LET'S PRACTICE

Think of at least three situations in which, looking back, you should have said no or given bad news up front.

- What was the situation?

_____

_____

- What was your intention when you said yes or set the expectations higher than you thought were realistic?

_____

_____

- What was the impact? (Was the other person disappointed, upset, etc.?)

_____

_____

- Looking back, what would you have done differently? (Even if you understand the negative impact that comes with not saying no, some situations are very difficult to confront. It will become easier immediately, but you have to start practicing.)

_____

_____

_____

_____

Spend this week observing how you and other Latinos around you avoid saying no when it would be appropriate or wise to do so.

During the next few days, practice saying no to simple requests even if you could actually fulfill them. For instance, a colleague asks if you could cover the phones over lunchtime. Say something like, "I'm sorry. I have a commitment at lunchtime. I won't be able to."

It will take some practice to get used to it, but once you master the ability to say no without feeling guilty (or feeling that you are not being nice or that you are letting someone down), you will feel less stress and you will actually cause fewer disappointments. If you are in a service job, you will probably lose fewer customers. If you are practicing

CAREER TIP

Always let colleagues, bosses, or subordinates know when you are not going to be able to meet an established deadline. They may be disappointed, but in any work environment there is more flexibility to push a deadline forward (if previously known) than to deal with the surprise of something not finished on time.

with your boss, you will gain lots of points as he or she learns that you are good for your word and that he or she can count on you when you commit to something.

You have a good predisposition and your tendency is to please your boss and colleagues. Do not let your need to please others get in the way of saying no when you cannot fulfill a commitment. If you do not turn down your boss or others when you know you will not be able to fulfill the commitment on time, you will be considered unreliable.

PROFILE
Ernesto Schweiker—The Voice of the Hurricane

Ernesto Schweiker arrived in New Orleans in 1970 from Guatemala speaking no English. To this day, he regrets never having mastered the language, which he believes could have opened many more doors and given him greater opportunities.

Still, Ernesto's story is quite amazing. He started off in the domestic side of the tourist industry, selling tours of New Orleans, but because most people did not understand that he was not a travel agent, they kept asking him to sell them tickets.

His wife at the time suggested that they take advantage of the opportunity and open a travel agency, which they did. That first year, they sold three hundred tickets. Then Ernesto decided to improve his chances by advertising on Radio Tropical, the oldest Latino radio station in New Orleans. Within a year, his sales jumped from three hundred to seven thousand.

After selling tickets for many years on the radio, he had established an excellent business relationship with its management, so it was not completely out of the realm of possibilities when one day, the manager who sold him the advertising space said he would not be selling him space any longer—because he had decided to sell him the station. The manager was afraid that when sold, the station would change its format and no longer broadcast in Spanish, so he found it natural to approach his biggest customer.

Not knowing much about the radio business yet excited about the opportunity and filled with a sense of responsibility to save the Latino radio station, Ernesto decided he wanted to take on the challenge. He flew to Guatemala and asked his family for a loan, which he paid back over the next few years.

In 2005, when the entire city of New Orleans was being evacuated due to Hurricane Katrina, this tenacious man refused to leave until absolutely every listener had left. He was also one of the first people to return. After he located the only generator available in the area, he traveled eight hundred miles to pick it up. It was a small generator, however, and it only had enough power to start up the transmitter. If they turned on any lights, the transmission went down. They broadcasted for days with no electricity and no water so that families in Latin America could find out about their relatives in New Orleans.

Ernesto talks about that difficult time as if what he did was the most natural thing to do. He was there to fulfill a mission and no obstacle was too big for him to overcome. His hard work driven by honest values paid off. Soon, businesses returned to New Orleans and they began advertising strongly on Radio Tropical in search of workers to help rebuild the city.

What possessed this man to take such a leap of faith? It has a lot to do with Ernesto's strong values and perseverance. He has always been moved to do what is right, and he also knows that if he perseveres, he can succeed at whatever he sets out to achieve, whether it is to sell tickets or run a radio station.

He had grown used to overcoming obstacles. After all, he had experienced them throughout his life in the U.S., when his lack of language limited his ability to progress in several areas. When asked what he would have done differently, had he known back then what he knows now, Ernesto does not hesitate. He would have had a road map for his future; he would have projected his ambition, because "in this country," he says, "you can do that. You don't have to act impulsively."

As is the case with most successful people, Ernesto has several traits that he has used to his advantage. He was flexible to try very diverse occupations even if it meant learning something from scratch; he was able to tolerate uncomfortable situations and used his creativity to overcome them; he worked hard his whole life; he is courageous; and, he has a strong value system that has always guided his decisions.

❧

The Ability to Build Strong and Loyal
RELATIONSHIPS

There are three key traits in building strong and loyal relationships—empathy (the ability to connect with other people's feelings and situations), effective networking, and strong cooperation. As a Latino, you have an innate ability to establish strong and loyal relationships. In the next example, you will meet Jessie and will have a chance to see the impact of these traits in action.

EXAMPLE

One day, Pedro was stranded at the La Guardia airport during a snowstorm. He had arrived very early in the morning to find out that his flight to Florida had been canceled. The airport was a mess. There were people wandering around trying to find information and endless lines of passengers trying to catch a taxi to go back to the city. Fortunately, Pedro ran into John, his boss, who offered him a ride back to the city in the car that was picking him up.

They were waiting outside when Pedro saw a big guy getting out of a black town car, smiling and holding two cups of coffee. It was Jessie, the driver John used every time he needed transportation. Jessie used to work for a bigger company that provided transportation services to John's office, but he provided such good service that many of his clients would request him specifically when making a reservation through the dispatcher service. One day Jessie decided to start his own black car service company, and with the support of some of his old clients along with new recommendations, he had managed to grow it slowly but steadily. In fact, he had been so effective at building productive relationships that his previous boss would also recommend him when he needed extra help.

After a few minutes, Jessie, who is from Colombia, had found out that Pedro spoke Spanish. By the time Pedro got out of the car, the two of them had had time to chat about their lives. Jessie gave Pedro his card and quickly became his choice of transportation.

Jessie's secret—one that is shared by most Latinos even when they are not completely aware of it—is that he is very effective at establishing strong and loyal relationships. He has practiced this skill not only with his clients, but also with his previous bosses, the drivers he hires, and the mechanics and car dealers with whom he does business. Jessie's story illustrates some of the behaviors that make him successful in his profession.

You know either through personal experience or through the stories your parents or grandparents told you that empathy, effective networking, and strong cooperation are all important components when building loyal relationships. These behaviors and skills mean a lot in your country of ancestry. It is quite certain that back in Latin America, it would have been impossible to achieve any goal without these skills. However, it may seem that in the much more structured and organized environment of corporate America, where everything is much more predictable and the system works (almost) flawlessly, you do not have much need to exercise your cooperation skills. After all, America has a tradition of making the individual the center of attention, and success is always viewed as an individual endeavor.

This combination of a technology-driven world and the efficient and impersonal American system may give you the false impression that there is a lesser need for strong personal relationships. However, your goal is to learn the importance of having ways to make others feel more trusting.

As a Latino, you have an advantage in doing this. You have learned this skill while growing up. You know how to make personal connections with other people—you have a built-in capability to connect with their emotional side.

EMPATHY

Listening and empathizing with others is a natural skill for Latinos. Latinos can usually put themselves in somebody else's shoes quite easily. That is why Latinos are so well-suited for service jobs like those found in the health care industry, the food industry, and in general, anything that puts them in contact with the public.

EXAMPLE

Regina is a nurse at a community health center. One day, a pregnant woman came into the Woman's Health department to see a midwife. The patient, Lindsey, was an American woman who could easily communicate with the provider. During the check up, however, Regina noticed that Lindsey was very tense, so she took some time afterwards to talk to her. Once alone, she asked if everything was okay at home and if there were any concerns she wished to share. Feeling

Regina's warmth, Lindsey relaxed a little bit and she shared with Regina that she would be a single mother and was terrified of the future. Regina calmed her down and offered to put her in touch with a support group for single mothers. She also gave her the name of the clinic's social worker with whom Lindsey could talk about the difficult times ahead. By paying attention to the patient's nonverbal communication, Regina made her feel comfortable enough to share some very private information. That, in turn, enabled Regina to help the patient in a way she could not have done had she not used her excellent listening skills.

EFFECTIVE NETWORKING

Effective networking as discussed here is not the same as networking within a corporate or professional setting. Here, it is focusing on the way in which Latinos naturally support one another and show that support by recommending each other to fellow Latinos.

What are people doing when they stress the Latino roots of those they recommend for various jobs? While they are speaking about established relationships, at the same time they are trying to give some assurances. They are saying, "I know these people, they share our values, and they will work hard for you because they want to preserve the relationship with me, and in turn, with you in the future." It is all about cooperation and it is through cooperation with others that you establish a strong network. You help others and in the future they will help you. This is the way all Latinos learn to function, either in their countries of origin or from their elders. Although Latinos are normally quite effective at building relationships and networking, there are certain aspects of networking that function differently in the U.S. Latinos feel quite comfortable within their cultural circle (that includes family and friends), but this effectiveness decreases as they move away from their comfort zone.

> ### EXAMPLE
> Carlos, who had just arrived in the U.S. a year earlier from Mexico, went to a Christmas party with his girlfriend, Andrea, who had been in the country for fifteen years. As Andrea talked with different people, Carlos saw that she was exchanging business cards. He took her on the side and emphatically expressed his disagreement with this practice. "This is a social event! You don't go around exchanging business cards with these people. It's in bad taste." His girlfriend was surprised. She had forgotten that this is not done in Latin America. She smiled and explained that in the U.S., a party was a perfectly acceptable place to network.

Learning to network effectively outside of the comfort zone of family and friends is important in order to achieve success in America. Chapter 8 is devoted more fully to the difference in Latino community networking and American networking, but for now, remember that you are a natural at recommending people who have a Latino background. Begin to extend your network beyond the Latino community to open yourself to more opportunities.

STRONG COOPERATION

Latinos all try to help each other, but as explained in Chapter 3, most reserve the additional effort for friends and family. Latinos know the importance of keeping their word and being there for those who need them. It is possible that a society that relies less on personal relationships, like the American society, has made Latinos a bit more reserved and probably less inclined to connect with groups outside their more intimate circle.

The challenge (and the Latino advantage) is to start leveraging your cooperation skills and put them to work more effectively outside of your own community. You are cooperative by nature. To take full advantage of your cooperation skills, extend them beyond your family and friends.

EXAMPLE

María works as an office manager and has lived in the same condo apartment for the past five years. She has a friendly personality and knows some of her neighbors, but only from occasionally running into them in the lobby or sometimes in the elevator. One of her neighbors who lives on her same floor had recently had a baby and seemed to be having some trouble adapting to the new situation. Every time María saw her, she looked very tired and anxious.

Although María is still single, she comes from a big family and she is used to dealing with kids. One day during an elevator ride with her neighbor, María said that she felt bad for her as it was obvious that she was not getting enough sleep. She shared some of her experiences with her nieces and nephews and she also offered to baby-sit. The result was a new friend in the building and someone else to count on in case of need. A couple of weeks later, her neighbor shared a tip about some interesting job opportunities at a company at which María had always wanted to work.

The Origins of Latino Relationship Building

Most Latin American countries share some similarities, especially when compared to the U.S. Regardless of what particular country in Latin America you or your ancestors come from, it is likely a place where institutions and the rule of law are not priorities.

Normally, rules keep changing all the time, it is very difficult to rely on services provided by the government, and the future always holds a good degree of uncertainty. For example, you never know when there will be a transportation strike, governments adjust the local currency on a whim, and it is difficult to do any long-term planning.

What is left when everything else is in doubt? Your family, your friends, your neighbors, and your communities. That is why Latinos all learn early on that when there is little structure in a country, the only way to subsist and advance is by relying on the people they know and making an effort to trust even those who they do not know. Because there is a mutual need, those relationships usually endure the passing of time and eventually become the most important aspect of their lives.

Clearly, there are costs associated with this kind of system. Trusting and cooperating do not always guarantee the best results. People are unpredictable and at times, being a trusting person can be painful. However, this is a small price to pay in order to gain some additional help to survive, progress, and succeed.

Now compare that with a system that works efficiently. Even with all its flaws, the American system offers predictability. The rule of law is a certainty and the institutions provide the services that they were designed to provide. For example, you can mail your payments because the post office works, the roads are generally in good shape, and the trains run on time. It is not surprising that this system relies less on personal relationships. There is no need to take risks with people you do not know well, even if it is more impersonal. For example, why try an unknown coffee shop when you can go to Starbucks?

Without a doubt, the most successful and efficient system is the one with strong institutions and the constant rule of law. Therefore, you need to make an effort to support this system. This seems to be what most of the Latinos who immigrated to the U.S. have done, by becoming law-abiding and respectful citizens. Some, however, have made such an effort to belong to the new system that they have forgotten many of the learned and innate skills typical of their roots, therefore wasting a great advantage.

Knowing that the systems in America are different than in most Latin American countries, you must keep your shortcomings in check. When it comes to relationships, there is a stereotype that Latinos will tend to make personal relationships prevail over rules or even the law. People also tend to think that Latinos sometimes take advantage of those strong relationships and can become less reliable. While this behavior was a necessity in your home country, in America, where institutions work properly and the rule of law is the priority, Latinos can find themselves in trouble by not adapting to and following the rules.

EXAMPLE

Many years ago, Albert was attending a training program with a mixed group of recent immigrant Latinos and Americans. During one of the activities the instructor asked, "If you knew that your wife had done something wrong (and we are not talking about a capital crime or anything like that), would you turn her in or not?" Albert remembers that the group of Latinos looked at each other with a baffled look, clearly thinking: "Is this guy out of his mind? What kind of question is that?" At the same time, one of the American participants said without hesitation, "Of course! She has to assume responsibility for what she did." Albert noticed that there was a big division in the room and that the Latinos were being perceived as a lawless bunch that would protect personal relationships over the law.

Although this example may sound a bit extreme, and many Americans would not think about turning in their wives, the truth is that for Latinos, any kind of similar situation would be open to little debate—relationships are very important and the law is, well, less so.

A different problem Latinos may face has to do with crossing professional boundaries when they feel too comfortable in their personal relationships.

EXAMPLE

Return to Jessie, mentioned in the example on pages 47–48. He became Pedro's preferred means of transportation when he needed a black car service. One night, Pedro was returning from Dallas on a flight that normally gets to La Guardia airport at around midnight. Due to some delays, the flight only made it to the airport at around 2:00 a.m.

When Pedro got off the plane he was a bit surprised not to see Jessie at the terminal and he called him on his cell phone. A very sleepy Jessie picked up the phone and apologized profusely. When Pedro asked him what he should do, Jessie suggested that he take a taxi home. You can imagine how furious Pedro felt.

It never became clear whether Jessie forgot about the pickup or just left the airport when he found out about the delay. It was also puzzling to Pedro that Jessie did not offer to get out of bed and go to pick him up. The one thing that became very clear to Pedro was that lately Jessie had begun to feel too comfortable around him. As Jessie was driving him back and forth to the airport almost weekly, at that point he probably considered him a friend, a fellow Latino who would probably

> overlook a minor slip. Pedro did overlook it, but there were consequences to this slip—Pedro felt less eager to recommend Jessie to some of his American colleagues. Yes, Jessie continued to provide a good service, but his reliability came into question.

Your ability to find, create, and foster personal relationships is crucial to your success. This innate ability comes naturally and should be used to its fullest advantage. However, as a professional in the American workplace, you must always remember to not take advantage of relationships to get out of previous commitments, engagements, and promises by thinking your fellow Latinos—or your good American friends—will understand. Learn to say no to those commitments you cannot fulfill before it is too late to back out honorably.

CAREER TIP

Make sure, even when dealing with other Latinos, that you understand the level of formality, or informality, of each relationship. There will be people (Latinos and non-Latinos) who will be very friendly and informal when talking about everyday things, and then become more formal when talking about business topics. Keep in mind that each individual has different ways of demarcating his or her area of comfort. Above all, remember that being friendly should never mean compromising your professionalism.

DO NOT TAKE IT PERSONALLY

One more thing to keep in mind in terms of building relationships effectively has to do with keeping boundaries between your personal life and business. Think back to the example of Marisol on pages 13–14, the woman who was sent to special customer service training for speaking too loudly on the phone about private matters at the reception desk. She thought that her supervisors did not appreciate her friendliness towards patients, whereas the problem had to do with her lack of boundaries.

Because of the openness and easiness of establishing relationships among Latinos, many do not make a distinction between private and business matters. Even when being friendly with customers is the secret of the success of Latinos in all service-related industries, there are situations when this lack of separation can become problematic. This trait may lead you to take business problems too personally.

EXAMPLE

Lidia is the producer of a radio show. Susana, the author of a recently published book on a key topic for Latinos, contacted her to find out if Lidia wanted to interview her for her show. Lidia accepted gladly, because she knew her audience would love to hear Susana talking about this important issue. She clarified that there could not be any mention of the name of the book because it would be considered too commercial. Surprised, Susana explained that she had been invited to several radio shows and that this was how experts were introduced to the audience—as the authors of such and such book. Lidia became offended by the implication that she did not know how to treat experts and turned Susana down. By taking the comment personally, she missed the opportunity to have a guest at her show who would have given her great content for her audience.

The Latino culture is emotional in nature. For this reason, we have to really watch the way we manage those emotions. In America, there is a more defined line between your personal and your business life. Business relationships—even when they are friendly—are clearly that: business. In order to be successful in this country, this is a very important lesson to learn.

The following exercise will help you work on not taking comments made in a professional setting personally, and it will also make you more aware of when other people take things personally. If you understand what is going through the heads of those making the comments, you can adjust your style to make things better.

LET'S PRACTICE

Think of an instance in which you allowed your emotions to take over during what should have been just a business transaction. (For example, you asked for a colleague to review your work and give you feedback, but then got very upset when he or she gave you the comments back.)

■ What was the situation?

_____

_____

■ What made you cross the line and take it personally? (Did you feel it was a personal attack? Was the language too direct?)

_____

_____

■ What opportunity was lost because of this shift to the personal level? (Did you miss some comments that could have improved the quality of your work?)

_____

_____

■ Looking back, what could you have done differently? (For example, if someone gives you feedback using harsh language, you can tell him or her how you feel, or you can ask a third party to review the comments and assess their validity if you feel you are too close to the issue to make an impartial assessment.)

_____

_____

It is important that you reflect on these situations and understand clearly the impact of your actions. Always keep in mind that with stereotypes, many people are waiting to confirm their perceptions and even their prejudices. Using other people as role models will help you see the situation from a different perspective.

To sum it up, on the one hand, your skills to develop strong, loyal relationships, to cooperate with people, and to network successfully give you an advantage in the American system. On the other hand, however, you need to consider all issues at stake when you value personal relationships over the rule of law in order to succeed in the United States. You also need to honor your commitments. The best way to achieve this balance is to learn when to say no when necessary and learn how to say it in a way that does not harm the relationship you have. You also need to make sure that you do not take things personally when they are business related. You might be turning down opportunities or closing doors that might be very hard to reopen.

PROFILE
Teresa Mlawer—Still Number One after All These Years

Ask anyone who is interested in Spanish books if they know Lectorum Publications, and chances are they do. Knowing Lectorum and knowing Teresa Mlawer is one and the same, because for the last thirty years she has dedicated all of her energy to making this company, originally only a bookstore in New York City, the largest Spanish book distributor in the country. And although Scholastic purchased Lectorum in 1996, the company kept Teresa as Lectorum's president. It could not have been any other way, because Lectorum is, in Teresa's words, "her baby."

Teresa came to this country from Cuba when she was 17, along with her parents. Having just finished her high school studies in a private school and needing to work to help at home, she found her first job at Macmillan Publishing. "They had a new manager who was interested in expanding sales in Latin America and they hired me because I spoke Spanish," Teresa explains while she reflects on the fact that she was never aware of the label "Latina." "There was little immigration from Latin America in the sixties and I never felt discriminated against."

You only need a few minutes around Teresa to immediately realize why she has been so successful in the United States. She will also tell you that, "since I was a little girl, I always wanted to be number one. I always had to be the best in class, and the best at anything I did. It has been like that my entire life, and it has no connection with money. My ambition has always been to give the best of me."

Granted, not everyone who wants to be number one achieves that position, but Teresa has two other key traits that propelled her through her career—she is perseverant and an incredibly hard worker. "I get people to work hard for me because I'm there working along with them."

She has worked hard for years to develop the Spanish book market in the United States, helping Lectorum go from a small bookstore to a publishing and distribution power house. At a time when bilingual education was only beginning in this country, Teresa traveled extensively through Spain and South America in search of materials that could help immigrant children keep their language while they learned English. "I guess that what helped me was the Latino warmth, because I made friends with all the publishers and we are still friends after forty years. Their children stay in my house and I have stayed at theirs. At this point, I'd say in some cases they are more my friends than my clients." As Teresa herself points out, this is a typical Latino characteristic because Anglos tend to shy away from such close relationships with clients.

However, this same loyalty that she both professes for her friends and employees and expects from them is what may have kept her a little too close to her company. "If there is one thing that I would change about the past, it is that I wouldn't be so conservative. I could have used the same ability to work and to get people to work with me on a larger scale. That's my only regret—that I could have extended myself beyond Lectorum, and maybe because I loved it so much, I didn't. Being the president of Lectorum is not the same as being the president of Coca Cola." This is a valid point coming from a woman who has always wanted to be number one and whose ambition has not subsided a bit through the years.

Teresa, who has been instrumental in bringing Spanish books to the U.S. when there were none, and who has translated some of the most famous children's books into Spanish, believes that Latino immigrants will never completely assimilate. "Latinos have strong cultural roots with their countries. Because of the proximity of Latin America, they go back and forth. I particularly see it with the new generation; they are interested in their children speaking Spanish." She points out that in places like Miami, everybody speaks Spanish. "If it happened there, it could happen in other cities. I don't think it will ever replace English, but even Americans are realizing the importance that their kids learn Spanish," Teresa shares, and then adds that at her bookstore there are more Americans purchasing Spanish-language children's books than Latinos. "That didn't happen years ago when I worked at the bookstore. That shows you that parents know that it's good for their children to be bilingual."

There is no doubt that Teresa Mlawer is a hard act to follow. However, for the many Latinos who have always had big dreams, she is the perfect role model. With strong values and the ability to develop loyal relationships, if you work hard and persevere in your mission, nothing can ever stop you.

5

FLEXIBILITY

Flexibility is a broad term that could mean different things depending on the context. Here it is used to depict the ability to adapt to multiple and different situations—to be able to play different roles depending on the circumstances. In other words, flexibility is the ability to be able to adapt to a changing environment.

Every day you hear how the world we live in has been changing at a much faster pace than that of our parents. It is quite easy to understand what people mean by this. Changes in technology, especially in the telecommunications area and the globalization of the economic production, have altered the way we think about the world—as well as the way we imagine the future. The world we live in today is much more global than it has ever been, and is changing at an ever increasing speed. This changing world requires professionals of every specialty who feel comfortable with the process, understand its complexities, and can even anticipate what will come next.

The United States is at the center of this process of high-speed change and Latinos can benefit greatly from it, because Latinos have skills and abilities that are essential to understanding, surviving, and even excelling in this changing environment. Growing up, most Latinos have had to learn multiple survival skills like translating for their parents or negotiating between their parents' cultural habits and the new ones they found in their adopted country. Knowing how to use them in your professional life can give you a great advantage.

Many Latinos were raised in complex environments in which they had to understand and deal on the one hand with the world of their parents or grandparents who grew up in Latin America, and on the other, with the world of their peers here in the U.S. Those who grew up in Latin America had to withstand constant instability in terms of governments, learn to survive through recurrent economic crises and inflation, and overcome the challenges of inadequate infrastructure. The economic aspect has certainly had a critical impact on every Latino's life, as this has historically been one of the main reasons people immigrate to America. Inflation, a key aspect of the economic dimension, has given Latinos a crash course in adapting to a changing environment. Seeing your income—the product of your hard work—depreciate every day forces you to constantly change all the decisions in your daily life.

In such contexts, being able to adapt is an imperative. Therefore, Latinos have developed specialized skills that are extremely valuable in the modern world. The challenge is to learn how to put them into action so that you have an edge in your professional life.

EXAMPLE

Jason has lived his whole life in the U.S. His parents immigrated a little before he and his sister were born. They set up a very successful restaurant in a Hispanic neighborhood, so they never learned to speak English well. For this reason, Jason became their link to the American world. When he was in school, he used to translate the teachers' notes, and as he grew up he also started helping with some of the business matters that required a good understanding of the American rules.

As you probably know, when you translate (language, habits, codes, etc.), there is not always an exact match.

Very often you have to find the closest one, which means you need to analyze, compare, interpret, and so on. Jason learned all these skills from a very young age. He also developed strong negotiation skills. For example, he had to convince his parents that it was not good for him as a teenager to spend his entire vacation time in Colombia. At the time, Jason did not realize that he was learning very useful skills for the future—he just wanted his father to let him stay in Chicago alone while the family was away in the old country. Still, the skills he developed to convince his family (showing the pros and cons of the situation, projecting outcomes, giving up something in exchange for something else, etc.) were the same skills he would use later in his professional career.

Today, Jason works in the purchasing department of a large manufacturing company. He is well known for his strong customer focus (he is excellent at identifying his clients' needs) and he is a skillful negotiator, getting the best prices for his company while preserving relationships with the vendors.

Jason has been able to be as successful as he is because he made the connection between the skills he learned at home and the skills needed to be successful in a work environment. While it was easy for Jason to move back and forth between his Latino heritage home environment and the American system he was growing up in, he was able to accomplish something many Latinos find hard to do. He was able to internalize the new rules without replacing his old skills and forcing his innate Latino traits to become dormant. If you look at yourself and feel that these traits have become suppressed, remember that they are still inside of you. All you have to do is find a way to let them out and then put them to use for your advantage.

In the following example, you will see how interpreting for the adults in your family, a common skill for people who arrived in the U.S. at a young age, entails enormous flexibility, as you are dealing with two different cultures and are adapting to each one according to the situation.

EXAMPLE

Juana was 5 years old when her parents moved to the U.S. from Puerto Rico. When she started elementary school her mother did not speak a word of English, so Juana translated during the parent-teacher conferences. She also attended an after-school program to get help with homework. Juana had to explain to her parents how important her scheduled tests were and the fact that they could not take her out of school before the school year was over to join the family on their annual trip to the Island. She found herself always explaining how things worked in America. It was not easy to be her parents' teacher, and many times their confusion frustrated her, but she knew they relied on her to receive that information.

When she grew up, Juana decided that she wanted to work in human resources, specializing in international transfers to the U.S. Without even thinking about it, Juana gravitated towards something with which she had a lot of experience—interpreting the American culture for recent immigrants.

ADAPTABILITY

Adaptability is clearly the easiest component of flexibility to grasp in terms of conceptual description. It is also the easiest to understand in connection to work. Big companies spend a lot of money each year teaching their employees how to cope with change. They hire training experts, change management consultants, and buy books and videos focusing on managing change and preparing employees for a changing world. Unfortunately, Latinos who have all these teachings embedded in their cultural DNA are seldom aware of them, so they too have to learn them on the job, just like everyone else.

Most likely, you or your parents experienced constant change in Latin America. Whether the value of the currency changed or any number of rules and regulations were modified overnight, the truth is that unpredictability was part of your upbringing or that of your parents. That sense of "you never know what can happen tomorrow" is still in you, and if you can recognize it, you will be able to apply it to your advantage at work. It will allow you to always be ready for any changes coming your way.

Certain behaviors reveal this attitude quite clearly. For example, you are likely to be more cautious about borrowing money, you have a tendency to prepare for the worse case scenario in every situation, you have trouble planning for the long term, or you still have a general distrust for the American system.

CAREER TIP

Very often Latinos have a tough time during interviews answering questions about decisions made during their careers. Part of it has to do with changing environments that have forced decisions on you and others, rendering you unable to plan ahead. You have to train yourself either to find the common thread that makes your career easy to understand for others, or to explain, in a very articulate way, how your decision process worked. Keep in mind it is your responsibility to explain your career—not the interviewer's to figure it out.

Does this mean that you are so prepared for change that you will not suffer during the next reorganization? Not really. What it does mean, however, is that you are likely to have more internal resources to survive than others.

LET'S PRACTICE

The objective of this activity is to reflect on situations that you or your family have faced in the past. You will see how the strategies you used to cope with these situations can be easily applied to experiences encountered at work.

■ Write down a life example that involved change for you or your family. (For instance, the last economic crisis, which forced some of your family members to move to the U.S. to live with you.)

_____

_____

■ List the actions taken to adjust to this change.

_____

_____

■ To what extent are these actions similar (and applicable) to the latest big change in the workplace (reorganization, job transition, etc.) that you or someone you know have gone through?

_____

_____

When it comes to adaptability, you should feel comfortable to show it as part of who you are. This is a vital trait in the modern world and it is one in which you have been trained intensively. However, when you talk about this trait during a job interview, you need to prepare examples that are applicable to the professional world.

EXTREME ADAPTABILITY

It is possible to take adaptability to an extreme by becoming too malleable and accommodating. There is a phrase that summarizes very nicely what happens when you become too adaptable: "If you adapt too much, you can have trouble remembering who you are." Remember that it is who you are and everything that you have learned before that has made Latinos so successful in America. When you combine the nonconfrontational style of Latinos with your ability to adapt to almost any situation, you could end up with the short end of the stick. So be careful to avoid situations where you are taken advantage of. Analyze each situation carefully and try to break it down in smaller pieces. Evaluate if what you have is a real opportunity or one from which you need to push back.

CAREER TIP

Sometimes being too adaptive means getting assigned to multiple and varied projects. It is always positive to show good disposition and openness to new challenges, but you also have to keep in mind your long-term career goals. In addition, building an expertise or an area of focus is always important in the American system.

LET'S PRACTICE

Sometimes your adaptability trait has become so entrenched that you cannot distinguish good from bad anymore. Use a friend, former boss, or mentor as a sounding board to uncover situations in which you are being taken advantage of because of your nice demeanor. For example, perhaps you are asked to stay late at work more often than anyone else.

Once you have done this, and you have identified which battle you want to fight, planning is your best strategy. It is important to prepare a script of what you want to say to your supervisor and that you practice it before having a meeting to discuss the issues. No topic is off-limits as long as you present it carefully and respectfully. Keep in mind that the longer you wait to speak up about issues that are bothering you, the more difficult it will be to keep your emotions under control.

Feeling discomfort is sometimes a trade-off for avoiding confrontation, one of Latinos' most prevalent characteristics, but putting up with discomfort for too long may derail your career—if not your life. It is crucial to learn how to manage the downside of your adaptability in order to make the best of this otherwise positive trait.

EXAMPLE

John, born in the U.S. to Mexican parents, had been working for Eric, his friend and boss, for four years. They had a great relationship because they had known each other since college and Eric trusted John completely. Eric, however, was the owner of the chain of optical stores, whereas John was only the operations manager.

As the business was very successful, Eric took frequent and long vacations, leaving John in charge of the company. Eric would then call at all hours to discuss business issues with John with total disregard for John's personal time. Although John was grateful for the confidence Eric had in him, he had grown tired of sacrificing his personal life with no other reward than a "thank you" from his boss.

For a long time he debated over how to set up boundaries that had never been set before, without disappointing his long-time friend. He liked his job and liked working for Eric—he just needed to build some time for his family and other interests he wished to pursue.

After thinking about it thoroughly, John realized there was no other way to do it but to talk about it with Eric. He asked for a meeting and politely but firmly told him that he had no problem coming into the office every morning at 7:45 a.m. but that he needed to be out by 6:00 p.m. He was starting to take some graduate courses a couple of nights a week and he wanted to be home for dinner with his kids. He suggested that they promote one of the store managers, so that when Eric went on vacation, she could take care of John's responsibilities and John could assume Eric's without adding an excessive burden to his already heavy workload. Eric felt the proposal was fair and they began implementing the changes shortly after their conversation.

CREATIVITY

Usually when you hear the word *creativity*, you think of advertising and art. To some people it is such a mysterious concept that they think it is one of those skills that you cannot develop—you were either born with it or you were not. Both are misconceptions. There is much more to being creative than art or advertisement, and creativity is a skill that you can learn and develop. (In the case of Latinos raised in Latin America, for example, the environment forced them to be creative in order to survive.) The truth is that creativity is mainly about conceptualizing something that was not there before, whether it entails overcoming an obstacle, solving a problem, creating a new product or process, or just improving one that already exists. This section focuses on doing more with less, finding new ways of achieving results, and providing a new perspective in a changing environment that requires a creative solution.

If you grew up in Latin America, you learned how to find alternative and creative ways to get things done. Whether it had to do with scarce resources or deficient infrastructure, Latinos were forced to become masters at creating solutions to everyday problems. There is a saying in some Latin American countries that goes, *lo atamos con alambre,* which translates to something like, *we'll fix it with duct tape.* The idea behind this saying is you can employ a short-term (creative) solution to help you get out of a difficult situation. This does not mean being lazy and not going all the way to find the best possible solution, but being resourceful and maximizing your current resources when confronted with a challenge.

Have you ever heard your parents tell you stories about the water being shut down, and how they learned to always fill up the bath tub plus a couple of large pots for cooking before they left for work in the morning, just in case? Even today, there are people who keep a long piece of string with a hook tied to the end so they can lower down a key from the fifth floor when the electricity gets shut down and they cannot buzz people into their building.

This is not to say that there is no creativity in the U.S. just because it is a rich and organized country. In fact, if your daily problems are taken care of, if the basic infrastructure works as expected, then you have a lot more time to be creative at whatever you do.

The sophisticated infrastructure of the United States does make people more prone to take a lot for granted. It makes it easier and more efficient to follow the standards and even not to think too much about the chance that things may go wrong. When the East Coast suffered a massive blackout in 2004, very few people had landline phones that were not cordless, so a lot of people were left disconnected for a day or two. Living in an efficient and organized country decreases the need for stretching our creativity muscles. It is very important that you do not lose your innate ability to create solutions, and that you learn how to present this added value to your employer so that you have an advantage over others.

LET'S PRACTICE

The objective of this exercise is to analyze and learn from alternative ways of dealing with different sorts of challenges. (If you have lived all your life in the U.S., you should ask your parents and grandparents to help you with this activity.)

■ Think of something you take for granted in the U.S. (for example, using the mail to pay your bills or even having a telephone line at home). Now think of that same process in your heritage country (or ask your family how they did it).

■ List the differences and pay close attention to the creative ways they had to come up with in order to overcome the failure of the infrastructure or the scarcity of the resources. (For example, they used the phone at the pharmacy nearby, or the banks invented automatic debit in order to pay bills securely.)

_____

_____

If you cannot think of any examples, reflect on one of these:
■ Complex bureaucracies
■ Inadequate mail or phone service
■ Unsafe taxi cabs
■ Regular blackouts
■ No air-conditioning
■ Unstable banking systems

Now think of work-related situations or challenges that you have faced lately. Try to use some of the same approaches to address them. If you work for a small company (or a start-up), you are very familiar with resources being scarce. On the other hand, if you work for a big company, you most likely face long, bureaucratic processes that reduce efficiency. Do you see any connection with the types of problems or challenges described above?

CAREER TIP

It is acceptable to use examples that are not work related when asked about a skill during an interview. Naturally, work-related examples are always better, but you can show that you have a creative side, even if your previous jobs have not enabled you to use it. For example, your experience dealing with multiple cultures could translate into strong customer relations skills, or exposure to places with weak infrastructure could allow you to show your resourcefulness.

Activating your creative self takes work and practice, but it is certainly worth it as the marketplace recognizes resourcefulness and creativity as key skills. There is a lot of money spent each year on training programs that focus on these topics. Often, the techniques they use to teach these skills are derived from experiences similar to what you or your family have gone through. For example, they put you in situations that force you to come up with alternatives to a problem. Self-confidence is needed to develop this skill. Remember that you can absolutely do it because you come from a family that has been doing it for years.

LET'S PRACTICE

Think about this: how could you apply your creativity to the American system? To get you started, here are two examples of things that were invented in Latin America due to scarcity of infrastructure or resources.

■ Given the inefficiency of the mail service, people usually paid their bills in person at the corresponding utility company. For this reason, automatic debit (from a checking account or credit card) came into existence much earlier in Latin America than in the U.S. It was a safer and more efficient way to pay.

- Due to high gasoline prices, companies came up with fuel alternatives years before that became an issue for Americans. Cars that run on diesel and natural gas are a common occurrence in Latin America.

Now consider some ways you can apply your creative thinking to challenging situations in your workplace. Remember, just thinking *there has to be another way* can trigger creative ways to resolve challenging situations.

_____

_____

_____

PLAY DIFFERENT ROLES

The importance of being able to play multiple roles in the modern workplace is closely linked to being creative. If you think about the job interview process, you will immediately understand this point. Regardless of what your occupation is, every time you go into a job interview, the prospective employer will try to gauge how well you operate in a team environment, how well you work with others, and how effective you are at creating and maintaining productive relationships at work. What people fail to realize is that teams change constantly and that on each new team, some aspect of the role you play on the team changes as well. This means that you are expected to work with many different types of people in different situations. Demonstrating your flexibility and creativity will help you establish your reputation as a valuable member of the organization who can play diverse roles when required. In other words, being able to play different roles is essential to a team setting—and a team setting is essential to almost any modern workplace.

There are several reasons why you are naturally good at playing different roles. For starters, you have been exposed to more changing environments (or at least to varied views of the world) than many of your non-Latino friends. Now put adaptability, creativity, and biculturalism together, and the result is someone who can view the world from someone else's perspective and approach problems from diverse points of view.

As with all of the skills and strengths discussed in this book, when applied in the appropriate mix, they provide you with a decisive advantage. However, there can always be certain problems when you use them in excess. At times, the ability to play multiple roles in a team environment can lead to an uncomfortable situation. Since you may be good at adapting and getting along, but maybe are not that good at confronting, you could end up in situations in which you are playing multiple roles, but not the ones you would rather play. The key to avoid this shortcoming lies in managing your desire to be accommodating and in being able to say no. (See page 40 for more on this subject.)

GENERALIST VS. SPECIALIST

Closely connected to the pros and cons of being able to perform multiple roles is the issue of being a generalist or a specialist. In America, specialization is a highly valued trait—one that you need to develop if you wish to succeed in this market.

EXAMPLE

Federico was interviewing for a position at the head-quarters of an American multinational company. He had been working successfully for this same company in Mexico for over fifteen years. In fact, his name had come up through a talent review process used to identify potentials in his company. One of the interviews, conducted by a corporate human resources professional, focused specifically on his previous experiences in the country and its applicability to the central office. Federico had been through many of these selection processes in Mexico before; he felt comfortable speaking about his successes and how he had been able to achieve a lot with limited resources and to resolve transactions that were completely new in the country. When the human resources professional probed to find out his main areas of expertise, Federico stressed how he had been successful at managing multiple and varied products and felt comfortable dealing with most (or all) of them. The interviewer insisted on expertise and Federico kept talking about his versatility.

Federico did not get the job. He missed a critical aspect of the American system—it is key to be a specialist. There were not doubts about Federico's potential but he gave the impression of someone who knew a little bit about a lot of different things but did not have an in-depth command of a particular area.

This was not a completely accurate assessment. What happened was that Federico grew up in a system that encouraged the ability to learn new things quickly and even the skill to wing it when necessary. In fact, he did have a particular area of expertise, but he had made big efforts to widen his scope and even bigger efforts to present himself as a multipurpose professional.

One of the challenges that Latinos face in the American system every day is that specialists are highly valued while generalists do not always get all the credit they deserve. The challenge for Latinos (especially those who were raised in Latin America) is that they have been brought up with a completely different emphasis, and they need to reframe their past job histories to highlight their experiences as specialists.

WITHSTANDING UNCOMFORTABLE SITUATIONS

Another aspect of flexibility is resilience. If you are marketing yourself as being flexible, this has to include adverse situations—those that you would rather not be in if you could have your pick. How you handle yourself in uncomfortable situations often is the most telling way to determine how you will handle yourself in times of less stress or when things are going the way you would like.

EXAMPLE

Edgar learned carpentry in his father's shop while growing up in Nicaragua. He was very skilled and creative. Although carpentry was the main service provided by his father's business, every now and then they got painting jobs, some basic plumbing, and even basic building contracts. The business had been expanding based on repeat customers asking for additional services.

When Edgar immigrated to the U.S., he continued to be a very skilled carpenter who could also fix a toilet, do electrical work, or paint a house as an added value, but what he really liked was carpentry and his biggest wish was to design furniture.

His good relationships with customers helped him develop his business. Edgar realized that he was getting more complex jobs that were not in his area of expertise and that he was less and less interested in doing. He really wanted to develop his talents on furniture design. He knew that mistakes in America could be costly, so for awhile he kept taking every job, but eventually he realized that in order to be really successful he needed to specialize.

Slowly, Edgar stopped taking every job offered, and told his customers where he would be focusing his energies and that he would love working with them on these types of projects. He also provided them with names of people he trusted within his network who could perform the work up to and even beyond Edgar's own standards. He kept his clients happy, set up future referrals from his network, and shifted his focus to what he wanted to do.

Very often, your ability to adapt to changing environments and your relative comfort and endurance in adverse situations have trained you to postpone what you want, and sometimes also what you need. You hurt yourself when you put things off for too long, but how you handle yourself during your decision-making process can often determine how easy your transformation can be. Had Edgar, from the example, continued doing what he was doing, he would soon be in over his head and outside his skill set with the jobs his clients wanted him to do. Plus, he was not doing what he truly wanted to do. By offering solutions that utilized many of his innate traits, he was able to really start doing what he wanted to do without sabotaging his chance at success by handling the transition poorly.

CAREER TIP

Latinos always like to appear willing and ready, but when it comes to negotiating job offers, this can be a problem. The fact is that job offers are handled very differently in Latin America compared to the United States. In America what you get is an offer—you evaluate it, decide if it is good for you, negotiate certain terms (if applicable), and then either accept it or politely reject it. In Latin America, in general, they just tell you that you got the job—there is no expectation of negotiation. The impact of this cultural difference is that sometimes Latinos do not know how to handle these situations and feel that trying to negotiate the terms of an offer could jeopardize their chances of getting the job. It is important to not allow your flexibility to get in the way of obtaining the best possible deal. It is always acceptable to ask about terms and inquire which terms are negotiable, whether it is the salary, benefits, time off, work location, and so on.

Americans have the reputation of a people who are very assertive when fighting for what they want. Latinos, in contrast, have been taught to delay what they want and are satisfied with what is available. What you must learn is to listen to your inner voice and to distinguish your original objectives from what the environment is offering you.

Similarly, when getting assigned to projects and tasks in your current job, always keep in mind how those fit with your career plan and goals. It is wise to take a moment to reflect on the reasons for accepting a new assignment.

PROFILE
Mario Bósquez—Flexibility at Work

Mario Bósquez, the first Latino news anchor of a major television network (CBS), was born in Alice, Texas. His parents and grandparents were also born in the United States, and some parts of his family are fourth generation Americans. Nonetheless, when you talk to Mario, he not only speaks perfect Spanish, but he feels Latino.

He recently published *The Chalupa Rules,* in which he makes a connection between the different symbols of the Mexican bingo game and typical Latino proverbs. The idea is to recover popular sayings that have helped generations of people in Latin America, so that Latinos raised in the U.S. can reconnect with their cultural backgrounds.

One of the sayings he likes best is, *No seas como pollo recién comprado* (something like, *don't behave like a recently purchased chicken*), which means that you should not hide in a corner and try to become invisible. Bósquez feels that in order to survive, many Latinos in this country tend to disappear into the background, but as he says, if you want to progress in life, that strategy will not work. Mario believes that keeping that proverb in mind has helped him many times during his career. It reminded him that he had a right to be in the States and a right to follow his dreams.

Although he says that being bilingual has always been an advantage in his career, he immediately clarifies that being Latino will open doors, but it will not keep them open if you do not perform as expected.

In Mario's case, he had no trouble keeping the door open. That is because he kept another proverb handy: *Siempre serás estudiante* (*you will always be a student*). This one reminded him that there is always something new to learn, something new to try. To explore new activities and responsibilities, Mario used his innate flexibility, a trait he considers key because it helped him establish a network, communicate with different cultures, work at different jobs, and cooperate with others in all sorts of situations.

Just like the mermaid, one of the Chalupa symbols that Mario appreciates most, who can live both in the water and on land, Latinos can swim between the two cultures in a balancing act.

Having a strong knowledge of the American system provided Mario Bósquez with the tools he used to succeed—flexibility and a powerful sense of the right to succeed.

PART 3

IMPROVEMENT
OPPORTUNITIES

6

COMMUNICATION

As with the other traits discussed in this book, it is important to be aware of how you communicate so that you can use it to your advantage and you can beware of possible shortcomings. This chapter looks into the different elements that make up the Latino style of communication, and gives you concrete examples comparing the Latino style and the American style. Neither style is better than the other—they are just different and they respond to cultural patterns. Knowing when to use your own innate style and when to bring it down or up a notch is a skill you can master. Becoming conscious of your tendencies and recognizing your own particular style is the first step in this direction.

INDIRECTNESS

In an attempt to avoid confrontation, Latinos tend to have an indirect style of communication. It is easier and more polite to beat around the bush instead of shooting straight and just saying what you think. Many Latinos not only act like this towards others, but they also expect others to do the same for them. They want others to be gentle with their comments as if they could not handle the truth. This can be a problem when others do not meet this expectation.

EXAMPLE

Mary, the office manager at a large telecommunications company, was to give a report, and it needed to be edited by her two recently hired analysts. She wanted them to review the report, edit it, and return it within a week.

When Alice, her American analyst, turned in her copy of the report, it was covered with red marker underlines and crossed out words had been replaced by others on top, and there were also copious notes in the margins indicating what parts of the report needed to be rewritten or moved around. Mary looked at it and agreed with most of her analyst's suggestions. She thanked Alice for her thorough job.

When Antonio, Mary's analyst born in the Dominican Republic, turned in his copy, it only had a few pencil notations on the margin. It pointed out a few paragraphs that needed some work and it suggested some word changes here and there.

Mary felt that Antonio had not paid much attention to her report or put enough time into it, and she asked him why he had used black pencil when it made it so easy to miss a correction. Antonio knew he had disappointed his boss on his first assignment, but he was not quite sure why.

What happened here? Why did these two analysts, who were given identical jobs, come back with such different results? Antonio allowed his nonconfrontational, indirect style of communication and deep respect for hierarchies to prevent him from providing crucial information to his boss. Because he felt it was not appropriate to correct somebody else's work (especially in red pen) and that he would be disrespecting his boss if he told her the whole truth about her report, he left his boss believing that he was not as good as his American counterpart.

Alice, on the other hand, made all her corrections immediately visible and told her boss straight out what parts required further work. She felt that was the best way to save her boss precious time. She also understood that when her boss gave her the report, she really meant for it to be edited, and she was not looking for approval or compliments.

This example illustrates a case of the indirect trait not being effective. Antonio's approach was perceived as not thorough enough and—judging by Alice's comments of how much work the report needed—not straightforward. Antonio's attempt to be nonconfrontational showed him as not being completely honest.

However, the nonconfrontational, indirect style is a very positive trait in situations where negotiation skills are required. In such occasions, a nonconfrontational approach usually gets you much farther than a direct one, as it helps the people involved to save face and find agreeable solutions.

EXAMPLE

Charles was upset because he received 10,000 promotional postcards that he ordered from the printer and they had been printed wrong—the photo on the front was fine, but to read the text in the back you had to turn the card upside down. He could have used them like that, but he felt the impact would not be the same and he also thought he should not have to pay full price for something that was not printed to his specifications. He would have liked to get at least a discount.

He called the printer and said in a very nice tone, "I wanted to thank you for your quick turnaround. The cards look really great. I was only wondering if there was a technical problem when you printed them."

"What do you mean?" the printer asked. "Well, you see," he replied, "the front is perfect but the back is upside down, so I thought...."

The printer looked the order up and agreed that a mistake was made. He offered to print and ship 10,000 new cards at no cost within two days, plus give him a discount for the next order.

CAREER TIP

Developing strong communication skills is key in today's world. You might be very talented, but if you cannot express your ideas clearly and assertively, your chances of success will be reduced. Be concise in your answers. Understand how much context is needed when you are telling a story or answering a question so that you are not perceived as having an indirect style. Work on your assertiveness. Getting the right level of assertiveness requires practice. Do not overdo it, but do not be walked over, either.

As you can see, Charles' non-confrontational approach to the mistake had a positive impact with the printer, who instead of getting defensive was able to find a positive solution that made everybody happy. As a natural negotiator, your nonconfrontational style provides you with the tools to be a problem-solver, a diplomat, and a go-between. Remember, however, that sometimes being indirect can be interpreted as being dishonest, not knowledgeable, uncommitted, and unreliable.

LET'S PRACTICE

- Write down a situation at work when you used your indirect communication style and it had a negative effect. (For example, you did not openly refuse to take on an assignment that you knew you could not fulfill because you did not have the required tools.)

_____

_____

_____

- Why did your style elicit a negative effect? Did your actions show you as an uncommitted employee, untrustworthy, or lacking backbone? Try to put your finger on how your colleagues or bosses perceived you, and write it down.

_____

_____

_____

- How might a non-Latino friend have behaved in the same situation? What would he or she have done differently? (For example, he or she may have stated politely but firmly that he or she could not take on that assignment.)

_____

_____

_____

- Compare the two styles and note the differences. Appreciate why the more direct style would have elicited a more positive response in the same situation.

_____

_____

_____

Next time a similar situation arises, try your non-Latino friend's style.

HUMILITY

As you have read in Mario Bósquez's profile on page 81, he lives by an old Mexican saying that would roughly translate as *don't behave like a recently purchased chicken,* which means that if you behave like a fearful chicken and hide in a corner, you will not get anywhere. As you read, he believes many immigrants hide like this in order to survive.

The reason for such behavior may have a lot to do with how many Latinos are raised. Latino parents and grandparents teach their children to be humble, and to respect their elders and superiors. A sense of belonging to the family, to a group, and to the community is always stressed over individualism. Moreover, given the influence of the Catholic Church in Latin American countries, a humble attitude has always been valued. It is a wonderful trait shared by most Latinos. However, this is the country of individualism, and there are occasions in which you need to shine as an individual in order to be taken seriously.

CAREER TIP

In today's global business world there are many interactions and meetings that happen over the telephone, including job interviews. The challenge is that it is harder to convey a direct, clear, and assertive style over the phone than in person because you cannot see the nonverbal reactions of the interviewer to your answers. Whenever you have to conduct any type of meeting over the phone, be prepared, take notes, and remember to breathe and pause before answering. An indirect style becomes even less clear and assertive when you are not talking in person.

EXAMPLE

Richard, head of the human resources department at a large publishing company, interviewed two candidates with similar experience for a position as senior editor of the children's literature department.

The interview with his first candidate, Gloria, who was raised in Puerto Rico, went well. Gloria had been an assistant editor for a competitive publisher for several years. She would bring the additional advantage of being a fluent Spanish speaker. However, Richard was not able to figure out if any of the authors Gloria worked with had been discovered by her or by someone else in her group. Gloria said things like, "We had a list of very innovative authors" and "my department won several literary awards." When Richard asked Gloria if she had any questions for him, she simply said no and thanked him for his time.

Richard's second candidate, Gregory, was also an assistant editor, but he worked at a publisher of adult literature. Although Richard thought that a background in children's books was preferable, Gregory made a better case for being the best candidate. He had two children, ages 5 and 6, to whom he had been reading every night since they were born. He loved children's literature and was completely up to date with publishing trends. He even offered a few ideas on what he would like to see published. Gregory shared with Richard that he had worked with several authors who became best sellers. He had also helped improve the turnaround time of books to bring them to press sooner.

Before leaving the meeting, Gregory asked his interviewer where he saw the children's literature department in five years, a question Richard appreciated because it showed Gregory's interest in the company and particularly in his department. Gregory then said in a very excited voice: "I really enjoyed this meeting and I want you to know that I'm interested in this position. I think I have the skills and enthusiasm you need to fulfill your vision."

Even though Gloria had a better background for the position, Gregory came across as a stronger candidate. Gloria, with her typical Latino communication style, avoided showing off her accomplishments and instead forced the interviewer to draw his own conclusions based on her humble attitude throughout the interview. As such, he inferred that she had not done much in her department on her own and that most of the accomplishments were either achieved by the whole group or by someone else. Otherwise, why would she not point out precisely what she did? In addition, Gregory came across as much more assertive when he asked questions about the future of the children's literature department and when he openly expressed his interest in the job.

Being humble may not only hinder an interview, but it may also limit how far you get in your career. If you want to be a leader, you need to show that you can lead. And for that to happen, sometimes it is necessary to let people know what you know, what you have accomplished, and what you have to offer. If you do not tell them yourself, nobody will do it for you. Remember, America is a country that values individual achievement.

CAREER TIP

When you face an interview, you need to train yourself to explain clearly your role in projects and tasks in which you have participated. It is not the interviewer's job but your own to show which ones you led and which ones you worked on with other people. Do not take credit for things you did not do, but do claim your successes.

As with the indirect style, there is a very positive side to humility. It allows you to be open to other people's ideas, comments, and even criticism without letting your ego get in the way. People who remain humble despite their success continue to learn from others and from what life has to offer them. They are usually the most beloved leaders.

EXAMPLE

Mabel, a Cuban psychologist who has lived in the U.S. for fifteen years, had finally achieved her dream of having a weekly TV spot in a well-known Spanish network. After the first show aired, she had a gathering at her house with six of her acquaintances—both American and Latino—and played the five-minute tape for them. She asked them to be honest with her and tell her absolutely everything she needed to work on. Over coffee, she took extensive notes on their suggestions that ranged from her wardrobe, to how she sat on the chair, to the content of what she said, to the speed of her speech. Mabel repeated the exercise one more time after the second spot aired. She took the advice seriously and improved on all the areas that were pointed out to her, making the spot one of the most watched on the network.

Being humble enough to replay for others her first attempt on television was courageous. Asking them to criticize her so she could learn was the ultimate show of humility. Mabel's communication style enabled her to hear what people had to say without becoming defensive. This gave her the chance to correct her mistakes early, and it opened the doors for success.

CAREER TIP

Research shows that people make a decision about whether they like you or not during the first few seconds they meet you. So, during an interview, offer a strong handshake and good eye contact; don't fuss with your hair, your shoes, or the pen you are holding; don't cross your arms; keep good posture; and, smile!

Using your humility to always remain open to listening to people's suggestions and comments without becoming defensive is one of your strongest traits, leading to learning and growth. Still, do not let your humbleness get in the way of the promotion or job you want. Assert your knowledge, your accomplishments, and what you bring to the table.

LET'S PRACTICE

In career-related situations (job interview, networking, résumé, etc.) it is important for you to talk about your accomplishments in a way that lets others know exactly what they are. The best way to become good at this is by practicing with friends and then trying the technique in your work environment. The following exercise will help you take the first step.

Choose a friend and invite him or her for coffee. Explain that you need to practice talking about yourself in professional situations. Then spend ten minutes telling him or her what you have accomplished in your career up to now. You can also talk about your accomplishments in your life if you have not been working for a while. Make sure that you refer to yourself as "I" and not as "we," and that you only talk about your own personal achievements.

When you finish, ask your friend to describe your career-related achievements for you. Hearing someone else give you this feedback will reinforce your awareness of all you have accomplished. Then, ask your friend to tell you things you have accomplished that you may have left out.

JUSTIFYING MISTAKES

One of the characteristics that most clearly distinguishes Latinos from Americans is the way in which they handle mistakes. Most

Latinos tend to make up excuses to explain why the mistake was made, or they look to others to distribute the responsibility. Americans, on the other hand, tend to immediately acknowledge that a mistake was made. Next, they find a solution, apologize, or reflect on what they have learned from the mistake. Then they move on. The impact of this behavior is that it makes communication more honest and direct.

Why do Latinos have so much trouble admitting their mistakes? There is likely more than one reason to explore. For starters, the macho culture impacts men in a particular way. It is hard for them to admit mistakes because they may be seen as being weak. Therefore, they seldom accept their responsibility openly.

It is quite likely that this reason overlaps with others, such as taking certain things too personally. For many Latinos, when they make a mistake, they feel that they are bad people. Admitting to a mistake is like accepting that you are a bad person. Some essential part of your being is considered damaged by the admission of a mistake.

In the United States, on the other hand, people understand that everyone makes mistakes once in a while. As long as you are willing to take responsibility for yours and learn how to explain what went wrong in a clear manner, you will likely be forgiven.

This trait is easy to observe in the way our countries are run. If you do not remember, just turn to the Spanish news for awhile. In Latin American countries, whenever something goes wrong with an administration, the corresponding authority always finds someone else to blame for it. People are seldom responsible for anything. After something does go wrong, they spend lots of energy in pointing fingers to no avail. It is very unusual to hear any sort of public apology.

In the United States, although representatives from the Democratic and Republican parties will differ with each other on all sorts of issues, when something goes wrong, the topic is addressed and the people responsible are identified, made to apologize, and removed from their positions. Then, the administration moves on. Granted, this is a simplistic way to look at governments and policies, but in general terms, it illustrates how differently the two systems work.

If you were raised in a Latin American country, or by parents who were, you are likely to be prone to make up excuses whenever you make a mistake. That can show you in a negative light when you are in an American environment.

EXAMPLE

Robert was a project manager at the technology department of a medium-sized pet grooming company. He was in charge of the development of a new website that should have been online a week earlier. He was called into his boss's office to explain why he had not met the deadline. Robert explained, "Joan didn't give me her content until yesterday and Peter didn't give me the pricing until two days ago. Now that I have everything I need, we will have the site up and running by next Monday." Robert did not admit that ultimately the delay was his responsibility (he should have made sure that his team turned in the materials on time) because he thought that admitting it would make him look incompetent.

Robert's boss looked at him in disbelief. To him, it was clearly Robert's responsibility to see that the project got done on time. He decided to take the project away from Robert and assign it to someone else in the department. Although Robert did not lose his job over it, he felt punished and he did not understand the reason.

Robert's lack of admission of any responsibility in the delay annoyed his boss. If Robert saw that things were not running smoothly, he could have anticipated that he would miss the deadline and should have taken measures to make sure the project stayed on track and alerted his boss so he could have adjusted his own schedule to release the website.

Not only did Robert not take any blame, but he did not even apologize for the mishap. He acted as if he had nothing to do with the website not being ready, and as if it was all out of his control.

What Robert should have done is to admit openly to not having kept his boss in the loop earlier, to not having managed his team's time frame adequately, and to having missed the deadline altogether. Then he could have offered the hope that the website would be ready in a few days.

Not admitting to making a mistake can be a big problem both in your job and at a job interview. Others will perceive you as arrogant and a know-it-all. They may also think you are not mature enough to admit your mistakes and move on. Justifying mistakes is never an advantage. When you find yourself ready to make up excuses, close your mouth. Humbly apologize for any mistakes you have made, come up with solutions, and explain what you have learned from the faux pas.

CAREER TIP

Owning up to your mistakes makes honest communication easier. The key is to concentrate on the learning. Your manager will usually forgive you if you show that you understand what went wrong and that you learned something from it. Denial is not a good indicator of learning.

LET'S PRACTICE

Realizing that you are justifying your mistakes is the key to changing your communication style to a more direct one where you can readily admit what went wrong and assume responsibility when appropriate. In this exercise, you will review your past experiences in dealing with mistakes and contrast them with your newly acquired knowledge.

Think about a recent mistake you have made in the workplace. (For example, you placed the wrong order and have to pay to return the goods.)

- How did you handle the mistake? (Did you admit to it? Did you try to hide it from your boss or make up an excuse?)

_____

_____

_____

- How would you have handled it now that you know how poorly it reflects on you to make excuses?

_____

_____

_____

Remain vigilant, and next time you make a mistake remember to avoid justifying it.

OFFERING EXCESSIVE CONTEXT

Have you ever found yourself listening to one of your Latino colleagues tell a story while you think, *please get to the point!* Everyone has been in that situation, but the funny thing is, many times you may be the one on the other side of the equation. Often when a Latino tells a story, he or she feels compelled to explain who is married to whom, who knew whom when they were kids, etc. Latinos have a hard time *making a long story short*, as Americans would put it. The long details regarding the social interactions are extremely valuable in Latino culture; these details show the connections with each other as human beings and make life interesting. It is no secret that Latinos share a culture of feelings. Drama is part

CAREER TIP

There are a lot of training programs that can help you improve your oral and written communication. They are normally identified as "action writing" or something similar. Keep in mind that this skill—knowing how to present your ideas in an effective manner—can be learned.

of everyday life and most would not have it any other way. However, when this trait is brought into the structured, rational, and efficient American system, difficulties are encountered when this over-sharing is not kept under control.

EXAMPLE

Shana, owner of a T-shirt factory, asked her sales manager Horacio if his weekly sales report was complete. Horacio, who had worked at the factory for two years, said, "Do you remember that last week we spoke about changing the format of the report to include present and future sales because you thought it would help your financial planning? Well, I don't have the figures yet because I was working on the trade show sales for the next six months and I realized that many of those sales fell through because they had to do with the new items that are indefinitely in back order. So, I have to rework the numbers and I don't have them yet." Horacio's boss was stunned by the long answer. She had asked a very simple question, and a yes or no answer would have been enough.

Horacio could have said, "I don't have it yet. I've run into some minor delays but I'll get them to you shortly." Then, if Shana had asked for further specifics regarding those delays, he could have explained that there were some orders that fell through because of the new items being indefinitely back ordered.

The need to provide context can confuse your listeners or make them impatient. It may also reflect on you as not being a clear thinker or a well-organized person.

In a social environment, providing details and context always makes your stories much more lively and interesting. This trait can help you build good relationships and establish networks. In a professional environment, listen to the questions people ask and try to respond as concisely as possible. Beware of providing excessive context or information.

LET'S PRACTICE

The first step towards becoming a better communicator is to be a good listener. In the following exercise, you will practice listening to your colleagues at work to try to mimic their style.

During the next two days, listen carefully to the way your American colleagues answer questions from their bosses or peers.

■ Take notes on what their answers are, and how long it takes them to answer.

_____

_____

■ Now write down the ways in which you would have answered the same questions, and how long it probably would have taken you to answer.

_____

_____

■ Compare both answers. Are they equivalent? What is different?

_____

_____

Now pay attention to the questions people ask you in the office. Figure out what they really want to know and try to answer in a very concise way.

It will be awkward in the beginning, but as you become accustomed to responding in a less emotional and lengthy way, you will improve your opportunities of success in the American workplace.

INFORMALITY

The way it goes in Latin America is that you can just show up at any of your relatives' or friends' homes without calling ahead and you will be well received. They will set a place at the table for you and they will be glad you joined them for lunch, tea, dinner, or whatever. Parties are not scheduled to last a certain number of hours and people are not expected to confirm their attendance because it is understood that they are going to be there. Nobody really expects their guests to arrive on time either. They will get there when they get there.

CAREER TIP

Whenever you provide employment references, let the people you have chosen know. Do not assume that they will be okay with it. Also, clarify your expectations on what they can and will say about you. This level of formality will help your references be prepared to talk about you.

EXAMPLE

Susan had invited her boss Jules and his wife for dinner at her house. She was preparing a wonderful paella. The afternoon of their planned meal, Susan found out that her boss' brother and his wife had arrived in town from California the previous day. Without hesitation, Susan asked Jules to bring his brother and sister-in-law for dinner. This spontaneous and warm reaction won many points for Susan with her boss, who was impressed by her generosity and ability to go with the flow.

CAREER TIP

Keep in mind that there is a lot of communication that occurs nonverbally. The way you dress, for example, tells a lot about yourself. In this regard, companies have very different rules (and codes) about dressing. Always try to find out if you are interviewing for a more formal company (banks, law firms, etc.) or a more casual one (manufacturing, retail, some technology). In any event, it is always better to err on the side of formality. This means suit and tie for men and dress slacks or skirts for women, only basic makeup, and little or no jewelry.

If you ever tried to work with suppliers in Latin America, you know you have to adapt to their ways. In general, the work ethic is much more relaxed. People do not take deadlines as seriously as they do in the U.S., nor do they live to work. There is a lot of room in their lives for family and fun, and many times a job can wait until the next day to get done. While globalization is modifying the way all countries do business, people who were raised in Latin America or who come from families who did have a lot of those traits and attitudes ingrained in them.

This unstructured and spontaneous informality, which makes hanging out with Latin Americans a lot of fun, is the same informality that many bring to the professional arena. In that area, it is not a trait that Americans particularly appreciate.

EXAMPLE

Clara had been working as a business analyst for a midsized firm for five years with very good results. She was buying her ticket to go on a one-week vacation when she realized that there was a much better deal if she stayed a couple of extra days. She assumed her boss would understand her reasoning and extended her vacation without first consulting him. Clara's boss understood the reasoning, but not the way the situation was handled.

LET'S PRACTICE

In order for you to become more formal at work, you need to start observing your own behavior and practicing in small areas. The following exercise will walk you through the process.

■ Write down a list of areas where you can identify yourself as being too informal (for example, the way in which you present your proposals to your supervisor or the way in which you set up meetings with your team).

_____

_____

_____

_____

■ Choose one to work on first. Write down the steps you will follow to increase the level of formality with which you approach that area or task. (For example, call people beforehand even if there is a slight chance you will be late to a meeting or party, or type your proposals on your computer and hand them over in a folder.)

_____

_____

_____

_____

■ Practice it for two or three days and write your observations. Can you see any changes in the way others respond to you when you behave more formally? As you become more formal in this area, you can then go down the list.

_____

_____

_____

_____

PROFILE

Esteban Creste—A Great Communicator
―ᴄᴠɔ―

"Perhaps" is one word Esteban Creste, news director of Telemundo Chicago, knows well. It is one he looked up a dozen times in the dictionary as he was reading the *New York Times* while trying to learn English. That was over twenty years ago, when he first arrived in the U.S. and employed the indirect communication style so typical of Latinos. Even though he now speaks English fluently, he still complains that not speaking it absolutely perfectly has closed some doors for him. "Americans think that if you don't speak English perfectly, you are not a winner," he says.

With persistence and focus on his goals, Esteban has moved through his career from reporter to news director, using his biculturalism as a big advantage. "I always believed that I was more sensitive to the interviewee's experience because I had a multicultural view of the world. Also, being from a different country but living in this reality gave me the advantage to see things from a distance and at the same time from the inside."

Yet the fact that he worked for Spanish media sometimes got in the way of interviewing celebrities who perceived his audience to be too limited. Some small towns made the access to information harder for Esteban and some politicians would not give him enough time for an interview. He learned to work around these obstacles, trusting that given time, people will give equal access to the Spanish press.

If there is something that Esteban Creste strongly believes, it is that most of the Latinos who come to this country bring an incredible work ethic. "We come from ancient cultures; we have so much to give." And by no means is he an exception. Having been promoted from managing editor at the New York bureau to news director in Chicago, Esteban works extremely long hours with a very high stress level. His success, however, is as much due to his hard work as to his ability to serve his audience and make the right decisions. How are tough decisions, such as which news to cover, made? "I have daily meetings with all my staff, I listen to their suggestions and concerns, and then I make the final decision. It's interesting because it's always a pretty subjective decision. But I think I know my audience and I also know what they have to learn about even if they don't want to." These meetings—which are at the heart of a news operation—are daily opportunities to hone his communication skills. The careful balance between being open to his staff's ideas and maintaining his assertiveness once he reaches a decision is the clear sign of a leader.

Behind every decision he makes there is a concern for the Latino community. He wants to help, not just with breaking news, but with concrete actions, such as when his team did five reports on a hole in the sidewalk until the authorities repaired it. This strong value system has accompanied Esteban throughout his career, proof of which is the fact that everyone who has worked with him or has been in touch with him respects him professionally and likes him personally.

That respect has not come as a consequence of him being nice all the time. "Latinos don't know how to say no to their bosses. They are afraid of telling them the truth. I always speak my mind. If I think their strategy or idea is not going to work with our audience, I just say it." This is how he finally learned the difference between perhaps and no.

Esteban has put many Latino advantages in practice to succeed in his career—hard work, perseverance, a strong value system, and the ability to establish good relationships to name a few. But it should also be noted that he has learned the American codes well, and his ability to assert himself, communicate well, and say no when it was appropriate, backed by his values and his work ethic, have gained him a special place in the news.

7

CONFLICT
MANAGEMENT

L atinos are well known for being a lively, energetic, passionate, and sometimes very emotional people. Generally speaking, when it comes to expressing themselves, they are less inhibited than others. However, this extroverted aspect disappears when it comes to dealing with situations that involve conflict. In fact, dealing with conflict is something with which Latinos do not feel very comfortable. On the contrary, many would say that Latinos would do almost anything to avoid a conflict, using avoidance as the preferred method to deal with it.

Conflict Averse vs. Unreliable

The challenge Latinos face is that the general perception of them as conflict averse people contributes to their reputation of not being fully reliable. Being labeled as not being reliable in America can have a very negative impact on your professional aspirations.

Overcoming this trait can be particularly difficult. Many Latinos share the same codes and can anticipate (at least most of the time) when the other person is committing to something and when he or she is only trying to avoid a conflicting situation. People tell friends that they will be at their parties, while perfectly knowing that it would be impossible to do so. The challenge is that America is a true melting pot, where there are dozens of different cultures interacting every day. Clearly, Latinos cannot expect everyone else to know their secret code of communication and conflict avoidance. Plus, some of the behaviors that are normal and acceptable to Latinos could have the complete opposite effect in a different culture.

Another idea to keep in mind is that relationships for Latinos are so important that, if pressed, most will choose to protect any relationship over reliability. In the Latino culture, it is often less acceptable to say no to someone than to say yes knowing that you will not be able to fulfill whatever it was you committed to.

Within the American culture, it is quite the opposite. This culture deals frequently with conflict and confrontation. Saying no is fine—it is even considered a sign of independence and strength. On the other hand, being unreliable is a serious offense. In America, you can say no or yes, but then you have to stick to your word and honor your promise.

At times your desires will conflict with other people's desires and your opinions will differ from those of other people. To advance your career, it is key to learn how to express your views and state your objectives clearly. If you want to control your destiny, then you have to be ready to fight for your goals. The problem is that the Latino culture does not put heavy emphasis on individual desires, while America has a tradition of focusing on the individual. Here you are encouraged to fight for your rights and pursue your objectives and your goals. It is crucial for success that you make your own decisions and follow through with them.

CAREER TIP

Understand where the limits are for Americans. Your boss can go out to a happy hour and drink with you while talking about sports, but the next day he or she is still your boss. Americans are very clear about this. Latinos sometimes get confused.

EXAMPLE

Joe was an accountant working for a big bank. His boss, Loraine, was known for being a tough manager but smart and hardworking. She was also not a big communicator, which intimidated some people on the team. Joe's performance was good, but he had not received a lot of feedback about either what he was doing well or in what areas he should improve. He felt that it was time for him to be promoted, but had never spoken to Loraine about this.

Feeling frustrated, he turned to his human resources officer for advice. The response he got was the expected one: he should talk to his boss about the way he was feeling and the expectations he had. Although Joe understood what he had to do, he also felt very frustrated about the whole situation and could not find the strength to speak up because he feared that the conversation would turn confrontational. He just kept putting in long hours and doing the best he could. Shortly after, he decided to start looking for another job and he quit. In fact, Loraine was going to promote Joe. He resigned only a few weeks before the official communication reached him.

Joe's strategy might seem familiar to you. For many Latino professionals, it is easier to just look for another job than have a difficult conversation with their bosses. They just cannot bring themselves to set up a meeting and ask for feedback, which could involve tense moments. Consider, however, that these tense moments are rarely as stressful as looking for a new job, which includes going to multiple interviews, learning the rules of a new place, getting to know new coworkers, and so on. What is even worse is that you may be setting yourself up for only lateral moves from company to company and never really moving up the ladder to the position you deserve.

CAREER TIP

Talking to your boss, especially about difficult matters, is always tough. Experience shows that, regardless of where you come from, planning the meeting carefully is the best strategy. If it is about something you think you deserve, such as a promotion or a raise, be ready to show examples of your contribution to the company. Do not get personal. Prepare a script with what you want to say and practice it with a friend. There is no one recipe to relieve the knot you will most likely feel in your stomach, but being prepared always helps.

Learning how to overcome this fear of facing stressful situations will take time and practice, but you should feel confident that it is a skill you can definitely acquire. The business world is full of successful Latinos who have learned how to combine their excellent relationship skills with an effective way of managing conflict. One way to learn is by observation, and America is a great school in which to learn this skill.

LET'S PRACTICE

Overcoming your conflict-avoidance instincts will take some effort on your part. Use this exercise to reflect on some past situations when you did not speak up and to imagine different outcomes had you done so.

■ Think of three examples of situations in which you had a different opinion than someone else at work and you did not say anything. Reflect on the situation. (For example, maybe a coworker suggested an idea you are sure will not work.)

_____

_____

_____

■ What was the rational explanation you gave yourself for your behavior? (Maybe the coworker has been there longer than you, so you reason he or she knows better than you.)

_____

_____

_____

■ If you had spoken your mind, what could have gone differently? (You might have been able to save the company time and money by respectfully pointing out the flaws in your coworker's suggestion.)

_____

_____

_____

■ Think of three actions you will take next time. Remember, we are not talking about arguing, fighting, or even an open confrontation (although those things might be necessary at times). This is just about acquiring a certain degree of comfort with the tension associated with a potential conflict—enough comfort to be able to express your views in a clear and orderly manner.

_____

_____

_____

LEADERSHIP AND CONFLICT

It seems that leadership and conflict always come together. If you want to be a leader, you will have to face (or be ready to face) many conflicting situations.

Part of being a leader is making decisions, choosing a path to follow, and influencing and persuading others. None of those things are possible without some level of conflict along the way. If you want to lead, you will have to get used to conflict and you will have to learn how to effectively handle it.

Furthermore, being perceived as doers and followers rather than leaders is one of the biggest obstacles Latinos face today. It is this perception that in many situations delays and occasionally prevents Latinos from getting to the top positions in America. While there are plenty of successful Latino leaders in the American system today, the number is not growing as fast as it should, given the huge Latino population increase.

For every Latino who decides to take the risk, face conflict, and grab the limelight, there are many others who, despite having all the necessary skills and motivation, decide to go for secondary roles. Too many times this is done not because you do not wish to lead, but because you fail to use your innate skills—which can turn you into an excellent leader—to advance your career. You can be a great leader. First, however, you have to decide that you want to lead.

Again, the reluctance to lead can be traced to Latino culture. American universities put a lot of emphasis on teaching their students leadership skills. From early on, students get used to working in teams, preparing projects, and then presenting and defending their conclusions in public. Being a leader is something valued and encouraged. This is not the case with most universities in Latin America. In general, the education system is much more content-driven and much of the work is done individually. There are team projects, but not to the extent you see in the American system. This emphasis on teams and team leadership continues into the American workplace, putting Latinos at a disadvantage over their American counterparts, who have experienced much more of this type of activity. If you did not study in the U.S., there is some catching up to do.

EXAMPLE

Anthony is a software programmer for a midsized technology company. He is very effective working in teams and has a reputation for getting things done. During a staff meeting, his boss asked for volunteers to lead some of the projects for the rest of the quarter. There was one in particular that Anthony was interested in (and was an expert on), but when the time came to speak up, he remained quiet. The project went to someone else. Later, Anthony approached his colleague and volunteered to be a part of the team.

Anthony felt that there were others in line ahead of him for that particular lead role and that his time would come. In the end, he did not want to rock the boat with his coworkers, and he missed a valuable opportunity.

LET'S PRACTICE

Whether you grew up in Latin America or were raised by Latino parents, you are likely to carry around many contradictions. Words of encouragement to get out there and *show them who you are* mixed with *you had better keep quiet* have been instilled in you simultaneously. The point of this exercise is to reflect on some of those contradictions, many of which you are not even conscious of possessing.

Think of situations you remember that illustrate your Latino tendency to take secondary roles (like the one on page 75). It is possible that the more removed you are from your Latino roots, the more difficulty you will have to come up with an example. Some of the specific things to think about include the following.

- What was the message given to you by your parents about how to behave in America? Did they encourage you to take risks, or to try not to make waves and just fit in? Did they encourage you to volunteer to lead school projects or clubs, or to let others lead?

_____

_____

- What were the reasons given to you for trying to persuade you in that direction? Did they say that your turn would come, or it was not that important to lead?

_____

_____

- Did you see a difference between what your parents taught you and what your friends' parents taught them? Think about the impact some of these messages have had in your career. Consider volunteering for the next project at work, or even approaching your boss about taking on more responsibility.

_____

_____

THE THREE PS

It is important to keep in mind how your upbringing and early childhood experiences can play a significant role in how you think, behave, perceive, and relate to others. If you are a second- or third-generation Latino whose identity is primarily Latino, and whose personal network consists mostly of Latinos, you should not be surprised at how complex the contradictions are between your cultural background and what the system encourages.

Even if you are someone who feels very comfortable in the American system because of the way you were raised, never underestimate those messages passed on to you by your heritage. Instead, be proactive and employ the three Ps—put together a plan, practice it, and then put it into play.

Planning

Planning is absolutely critical whenever you are facing situations of conflict in which your emotions can take over. You should plan:

- before that big meeting with your boss;
- before a group meeting in which you want to express your point of view; and,

■ before a presentation that you are giving or attending (especially if you would like to state your views).

Do not take planning lightly. You should prepare for each and every detail, even write a script for what you want to say (statement, question, etc.), and anticipate questions you might be asked.

Practice

Once you have your plan ready, you need to practice it in front of other people so that you are ready for the reactions you might get. You can ask whoever is helping you to be confrontational, to push back, and to question your views. Nothing can replace practice for being ready and putting your plan into play.

Play

Once you have planned it and practiced it, then you have to do it. Remember that if you do not take that final step—if you do not take the risk of speaking up—nobody will ever know what you think.

The key is to start small and keep growing from there. You do not need to wait for a big meeting or any other important event. In fact, it is best that you do not try out a new interaction style in a situation that could define your career and your future. If you start with very small steps, practicing with situations in which there is not that much at stake, you will gain the necessary comfort and self-knowledge that you will need when you are faced with more stressful situations. So, the next time you have a chance, practice asking for clarification on a point with which you do not agree or politely but firmly express your different point of view.

COMMUNICATION

The Latino way of dealing with conflict has an impact on communication style. Chapter 6 was devoted to talking about communication style, but it is important also to discuss this topic here.

You may wonder why these two issues have to be covered together. Simply, conflict happens during interactions amongst people, and interactions happen via language. To top it off, consider that for many Latinos, there are at least two language barriers to overcome—English and Spanish—and that many of the interactions experienced daily are between two or more cultures.

There are multiple dimensions to analyze in the *Spanish variable*. Some of them have to do with the language itself. Spanish is less straightforward in general, and compared to English, uses more words to communicate any message. Clearly, the influence of Spanish in your life is a function of how long ago you or your family immigrated to the U.S. However, at whatever point your family learned English, while Spanish was still your family's mother tongue, it is likely that they have always used English in a softer, less assertive way, when compared to someone born and raised in an American family. This is the communication style that you have learned growing up.

You can argue, naturally, that you are so assimilated by now that these language influences are minimal. However, remember that during situations of conflict, emotions are heavily involved, and when this happens, everyone instinctively goes back to the basics. When it comes to communication style, you most likely go back to what you learned growing up. What is the impact of reverting to what you learned growing up?

- You might be using too many words to get the message across. Sometimes this is done to soften the blow when communicating something difficult.
- Your message might be diluted by your lack of assertiveness, such as when your boss agreed to something but then the actions do not coincide with this agreement.
- You might not be getting what you deserve because you are not communicating your desires effectively. This could mean setting limits or asking for something you want, like a well-deserved raise.

LET'S PRACTICE

When you are faced with stressful situations in your job, it is easy to hide behind your less assertive communication style to avoid conflict. Use this exercise to reflect on instances in which your communication style got in the way of getting something that you wanted or needed. It could be when you wanted something—a salary increase, a project, etc.—and instead of asking for it directly, you gave indirect signals, or when you had a good idea but you were not able to convey it effectively.

■ Write down one of those situations.

_____

_____

■ How did you craft the message? (How did you express your interest, your idea, or your desire?)

_____

_____

■ What was the outcome?

_____

_____

■ What do you think went wrong?

_____

_____

■ How could you employ the three Ps next time to get the outcome you desire?

_____

_____

The purpose of this section was to make you aware of your own communication style and to help you identify what happens to it during stressful situations. How do you overcome this obstacle and mitigate the impact it could have on your career and on your life? Go back to the three Ps—planning, practicing, and playing. Using them is the way to succeed. Most importantly, start small and build from your successes.

PROFILE
Cecilia Gutiérrez—Queen of Determination

Cecilia Gutiérrez has made it in this country out of sheer determination. She might think that her jovial demeanor was the key to landing her a job twenty years ago as personal chef of Peggy and David Rockefeller, but that just opened the door. Having clear goals, perseverance, and complete reliability were the skills that helped her not only stay in their employment, but also become the manager of three of the Rockefellers' homes. Her determination has helped her resolve many conflicts in her professional life, from needing to learn English to establishing her own nonprofit organization.

Cecilia's story is filled with examples of barriers that were overcome by her determination. She says that one of the largest obstacles Latinos face in this country is other people's disbelief in their ability to do something. "Nobody believes you can do it until you do it and you prove them wrong. We have to show Americans that we have the same abilities they do. What happens is that we are shy and we are afraid to show who we are. That is a big barrier we need to overcome. We need to show our values and our abilities to move forward."

Her subtle but assertive style has always been an asset not just in her work for the Rockefellers, but in her expansion into another, very different area. Several years ago, Cecilia founded a nonprofit organization that advocates for day laborers' rights, where she spends a large portion of her time giving back to the community. Being able to live between the world of the wealthy and the world of the extremely poor is a tribute to her Latino flexibility and to her determination to do whatever it takes to right a wrong. It is also a testament to her assertiveness—she has keenly used her access to some of the richest families in the country to organize fundraisers to bring gifts to poor children in Colombia. "The only way to succeed in this country is by getting very involved in the American culture, and I don't just mean to learn English, but to learn what this culture is all about, what the reasons are for this country to be the most powerful country in the world."

Cecilia's commitment to both the Rockefellers and to her nonprofit organization has guided her years in the U.S. Being clear—with herself, her bosses, and her dependents—about her abilities and limitations regarding these two areas of her life has enabled her to remain reliable. This clarity assisted her in resolving conflicts.

When she thinks about what she would have done differently she says she would have studied more—even though she got a business degree and attended culinary and nutrition classes. Beyond studying more, her advice to others is to "always move forward, always move forward. Never take steps back."

Cecilia has done much more than just learning the American culture. She has learned the codes of the American system extremely well and at the same time she has managed to keep her innate advantages in the forefront. Cecilia is an example of a marriage of these two systems as seamless as the perfectly served meals she organizes daily for the likes of Nelson Mandela and the Rockefellers.

NETWORKING

In the first part of the book, we talked about what it means to be a Latino and the value you bring to the workplace in terms of diversity. Then, we identified various attributes that Latinos have, including relationship building skills, a solid value system, and flexibility. In this third part of the book, we have been looking at your conflict management and communication styles as opportunities for improvement. Managing these two areas well is critical to your success at networking, one of the most important activities you need to develop in order to advance your career.

In order to ace networking, you will need to apply all the advantages your Latino background gives you, while keeping an eye on the drawbacks those same traits can sometimes contain. Latinos are wonderful at networking among themselves, and at networking socially with Americans. The problem is that many Latinos find it difficult to identify the goals of networking and use this activity for true career advancement.

LET'S PRACTICE

Before looking at what networking entails, a simple exercise to help identify the differences between networking among Latinos and networking among Americans is in order.

▪ Write down the people you consider contacts. Do not just write the names, but also their occupation or relationship with you. (For example: Marta Juárez, cousin.)

_____

_____

Ask an American friend or colleague who has a substantial network to do the same. Compare the number of people on your lists.

Analyze the following:

▪ What type of people did your friend consider contacts that you did not?

_____

_____

▪ What was your rationale for not including those people on your list?

_____

_____

▪ Look again at your list of contacts and that of your American friend or colleague. Can you think of people in different categories that you could network with? (For example, professionals you see regularly like your doctor, your accountant, people in industry associations, etc.) Write them down.

_____

_____

Now answer these questions and continue to add more people to your list.

- If you have children, could you network with the parents of their friends?

_____

_____

- If you attend church or temple, could you network with the other parishioners? What about the priest or rabbi?

_____

_____

- If you volunteer, could you network with the other volunteers in the organization?

_____

_____

- If you went to school or took courses in the past, can you contact old peers or professors?

_____

_____

- If you belong to any particular committee, could you network with the other members?

_____

_____

You now have a much more significant networking pool from which to work.

Despite their friendliness, Latinos tend to stay within a small circle of friends and relatives when it comes to making contacts. This limits your ability to grow and progress in your career. As you probably have noticed with the exercise you just did, your American friend had a lot more names on the list than you did.

In Latino culture, doing business at social events is seen as rude. You will rarely see guests exchanging business cards at a Christmas party, for example, whereas in this country that is a common practice. It is a relaxed atmosphere, everyone is having fun, you talk to people about what they do and what you do, and soon enough you find that you can help each other. If you can keep your internal judge aside (the one who tells you that what you are doing is impolite), you can enjoy the party and at the same time make some connections.

However, keeping business out of the social realm is not the only obstacle Latinos face when it comes to networking. Being such a people-oriented group, it is hard for Latinos not to take things personally when someone turns them down. For that reason, many times even when you overcame the first barrier and you actually befriended others outside of your tight circle of friends and family, you may avoid asking for something specifically—a business contact or a recommendation—just so that you do not have to confront rejection. Even at social events, business is just business, so do not take things personally if you approach someone for a business contact and are turned down.

At this point, it is crucial to understand that you should never take things personally when they relate to your career. Good networking requires establishing relationships and being prepared to encounter some people who will not show much interest in you or what you have to

CAREER TIP

It is estimated that 70%–80% of jobs are filled by people who heard about a particular position through word of mouth. Now you understand why if you are looking to advance in your career, you have to expand beyond your close-knit family. You have to stop spending most of your time on the Internet and you need to get out there to meet some people. Talk to everyone you can. Get used to making cold calls. Walk into meetings where you do not know a soul and talk to people. Ask your friends and colleagues to introduce you to their contacts. Networking can be threatening, but if you remember how deft you are at establishing strong and loyal relationships, you should have no problem.

offer. It entails dealing with contacts who do not take your phone calls or return your emails, or who ask you to call back time and again. It basically means that you have to be able to deal with people saying no to you. None of this should discourage you, because it is not done to hurt you. It is just the way things work. If you expect to encounter people who are not interested in what you have to offer or in listening to you, you will save yourself a lot of disappointment because you will be prepared. Part of this preparedness is understanding some basic rules of networking.

Who is a Contact?

By now, the statement that you need to expand your contacts beyond your family and friends may be acquiring meaning for you. The idea is for you to realize that a network is basically a chain—you become friendly with people who may know people who may know more people. The more people you know and the more people who know you, the more chances you have of moving up in your career.

If you grew up in Latin America, you should also keep in mind that you have not attended school in this country. Given that those formative years are when people meet many of their contacts, you have a lot of catching up to do.

The idea is to start thinking about the world in a different way. Besides just having your close friends and family, you must develop countless other relationships that will function as your safety net, because whenever you wish (or need) to move in your career or to develop a new project, these contacts will help you do it faster and better. They are the key to opening doors.

The Latino community is a great group for networking with, because they naturally try to help each other. It is a well known fact in the human resources field that some communities are better than others at collaborating with each other professionally, and Latinos are one of the better ones. If you hire a Latino in any given position, within a few years you will likely have a whole bunch of Latinos working in that department or company, which does not happen with all communities. It happens among Latinos because they possess traits that make them ideal candidates for successful networking. You just have to learn to network both with Latinos who are outside of your family and friends as well as with non-Latinos. The goal is that if you learn how to be a strong networker you will build strong networks, which in turn will propel you to key positions.

Basic Rules

If you think of networking as making friends, you will realize that you are perfectly equipped to succeed at it. That is what it really is all about. You need to care for people and see how you will be able to help them before you even think of how they can help you. This should become second nature to you; it should be something you do effortlessly all the time. There are only a few rules that you must follow in order to do it smoothly and with the best results.

The first thing you need to be aware of is that networking involves work. You have to go places, organize events, participate in activities, call people, send them information they need, and constantly follow up. If you do it as a way of life, you will develop long-lasting relationships that in the long run will help your career and the quality of your life.

At different times, however, you will need to use or expand your network for different reasons. To do this successfully, you have to prepare yourself in several areas. For starters, you have to be clear about what you are looking for. For instance, are you looking to change jobs? What are your qualifications and desires for your new career move? Do you just want to meet people to open your horizons? What will you tell them about yourself?

Be prepared to talk about your background and experience. What is your expertise? How do you describe yourself? Having an executive summary of your experiences is a must. You should be able to describe yourself briefly and effectively, while at the same time you should be able to adapt your script to your audience.

It is important to remember to bring your business cards with you wherever you go. Business cards provide the contact information needed to follow up and to remind potential resources of who you are. Failing to bring and hand out business cards when you meet relevant people forfeits your chances of making some great contacts.

Part of networking is the effort it takes to establish new contacts. Many times, when you have set your sights on someone you would like to meet, it can be very frustrating to realize they are unreachable. Those are the ones you should try hardest to reach, because everybody else suffers the same frustration and only those who persevere will succeed in reaching these contacts.

The other thing to keep in mind is that there is a fine line between networking and hard selling. You definitely do not want people to run away from you every time they see you because they feel you are trying to sell them something, whether it is a project or a product.

When you engage in different networking opportunities (such as special events, parties, conferences, and so on), use your innate charm and make sure that you find out as much information about the other person as you are sharing about yourself. One of the big secrets of good and rewarding networking is that it is an exchange. It may not be symmetric because the give and take may not happen simultaneously, but there is an unspoken understanding that the exchange will take place at some point. The key is to always give first. Be extremely generous with your new friend; find out first how to help him or her achieve any of his or her dreams. Offer to connect this contact with people you know who could be helpful to him or her and make the phone call on his or her behalf.

If you grew up in Latin America, you have been exposed to this side of networking even though you may not be aware of it. How many times have you said to a friend, "I'm going to give you Jorge Pérez's number. Tell him I referred you to him. He owes me a favor." In a way, networking is about the constant flow of favors. There is one big caveat—you should never keep score. You should be ready to give as much as you can to each one of your contacts just as you give to your friends. You will be amazed by the results.

EXAMPLE

Josephina, a children's therapist, met Carly, the Director of English as a Second Language of a large school district, at a party. They were talking about the need for parents to learn more about their teenagers' sexuality, an issue in which Josephina specialized. Before the night was over, they exchanged cards and Carly promised to call with the name of a contact person. A week later, she called with the name of the social worker in charge of organizing workshops, Harriet.

Harriet told her about the numerous parenting programs and shared the incredible success they were having. Josephina's workshops would be a great addition to their ongoing efforts to attract more parents to the schools. She arranged for a series of sessions to be conducted at all the schools in the district, awarding Josephina quite a large contract.

Right after her conversation with Harriet, Josephina called Gladys, a journalist who had interviewed her a few weeks earlier, and shared with her the story about the school district's programs. She suggested that she might want to write an article about their success with parent involvement. Gladys was grateful for the tip and promised to call the following morning. Josephina then called Carly and in addition to telling her about the contact with Harriet, she told her that the journalist would call her the following day.

What you see in this example is how at a friend's party, Josephina benefited from meeting Carly, who in turn introduced her to Harriet, who hired her for the workshops. You also see how she right away thought of offering positive publicity to the district, which is positive to both Carly and Harriet. She also provided Gladys with a good story, something journalists are always hungry for, and that way she is returning Gladys's favor of interviewing her.

One more thing you should take away from this example—Josephina's call to Carly updating her on the contract to give workshops for Harriet. It is always a great idea to keep your contacts in the loop when they refer you to other contacts. People naturally like to be helpful and they appreciate being recognized for their good deeds.

LET'S PRACTICE

Prepare yourself to talk to people about you in an interesting and appealing way. What you say to people you meet for the first time will probably vary depending on the stage of your life and your career. Adjust your presentation to your circumstances.

Think about the main aspects that define who you are, what you know, where you have been, and what you bring in terms of value. Do not focus only on your professional side—think of your hobbies, interests, and anything that says something about you that can help you make a connection with someone else. Remember that networking means making friends and connecting at a human level with someone.

Prepare different versions of your presentation to be used in different situations—a shorter one (usually known as the *elevator speech*) that you should be able to cover in one to three minutes, and another, more detailed, one that can be more flexible. You can type this speech on a card to hand out when you are networking for a new job.

An example of an elevator speech that you would use if you were looking for a job follows.

"I am a medical secretary with four years' experience in an MD's office. I am proficient in Microsoft Word, Excel, PowerPoint, Access, and Outlook. Most recently I worked for Doctor Ricardo Pereyra's dental office in Mexico City, Mexico, where I was noted for exceptional phone skills and for handling pressure calmly. I have received bonuses for my contribution to office efficiency. I have learned that I have the professional skills to work as a personal assistant. I am bilingual."

Following is a speech you would use if you were just socializing at an event, trying to meet new people to add to your network.

"I live in New York. I'm a medical secretary at a pediatrician's office in Jackson Heights. It's a great place and I get to do what I love most, which is to be around kids. I don't have any of my own, so for me it is great. I try to keep them calm and entertained so they don't cry. I play with them, read them stories...all this in between answering the phones and making appointments. It's really busy, but most of the time it's a lot of fun!"

Create your own speech and then practice it with friends and family until you feel comfortable.

Another basic rule of networking—and perhaps the most important one if you want to succeed—is following up. Nothing will happen if you do not keep up with your new friends. You need to stay in touch, provide information they find useful, make contacts for them, update them on your own progress, invite them to special events, and so on. Many people attend multiple events a year and pick up business cards right and left, only to throw them into their desk drawer and forget all about the people they met. That is not networking. If you cannot recall people who gave you a card, it means you did not spend quality time with them. You did not find out what their interests are, what they do, or what their goals are. If you cannot do that, the card is worthless. So, right after you meet someone, write notes on the back of his or her card to remind you about things you promised to send, people you promised to talk to on his or her behalf, and so on. Then follow up!

Great Places to Network

Now that you are seeing the bigger picture, it is important to think about a few places where you get the opportunity to network with a lot of people at a time. Depending on your area of interest, you will have different options. You can start by joining Hispanic organizations, but do not stop there. Other logical places for you to start include professional associations, industry shows, meetings of the local chamber of commerce, conferences, workshops, committees at work, company boards, and job fairs. These groups and situations offer you an environment where there are lots of people from your industry under one roof.

The secret is to be able to approach people politely but assertively to exchange ideas, common interests, possible synergies, and business cards. If you remember that most of the participants in those meetings are there because they are networking, you will not feel out of place doing it yourself.

Networking in Practice

To network successfully, it is important for you to focus on why others will remember you. You meet many people every day, so think about this: What makes you stand out from the rest? Is what you have to offer really *that* unique? Even if it is, people are likely to forget you if there is nothing attached to you, your product, your service, or your pitch.

Look at the following scenario. Say you have written a book and you need to publicize it. You do your research and get in touch with reporters and radio and television producers in hopes of them interviewing you. If your plan is to write more books, you will likely need to contact the same people when your next title is out. What should you do to stay within these people's radar until then?

If you take the time to study the media business, you will soon find out that it is hungry for ideas. Every day all the television networks, newspapers, radios, and Internet sites are desperate for new and fresh content. If you have good ideas, even if they are not about your books, they are a valuable commodity for you to share with these producers. You already have access to these producers; therefore, you should feed them information they could use. Feeding the network is a key you should always remember. For example, in this case, providing ideas for shows or articles gives you a perfect reason to stay in touch with the people who will help you again down the line. You may want to start writing articles about your topic of expertise and publish them in papers. Not only will you continue to get your name out there, but you will continue to develop relationships in the industry. You will slowly become an insider.

CAREER TIP

Informational interviews are a good way of networking. If you are interested in getting into a new field, you can ask people already working in that field for an informational meeting. Since there is no pressure for an actual job offer, these are normally more relaxed for both parties. This could lead to good contacts for the future.

Keeping in mind that networking is about developing relationships, you should spend time with your connections and you should learn about them as much as you can. Where are they in their careers? Are they happy? Do they wish to change jobs? The more you know, the better positioned you will be to help them.

For instance, you find out that Margaret, who works at CBS, would like to find a job at Univision, and you know that John, a senior producer at Univision, is looking to hire new talent. Naturally, you put them in touch. By helping people with their own careers and personal issues, you will find yourself in the center of the action. Suddenly, you are not "just" another author (or whatever your profession is)—you are a mover and shaker. You are someone who makes things happen for others. You not only take, you give, and you hopefully give more than you take. This rule is at the heart of effective networking.

Networking has so much value for your career. It helps propel it forward, because it opens doors when you need them, allowing you to fulfill your dreams. Remember, networking is always a two-way street. The day you forget to return people's phone calls or to help someone who needs you is the day when the doors will begin to close for you too. Just as you seek access, so do others.

LET'S PRACTICE

Besides knowing who you are and what your goals are, to strengthen your networking abilities, it is also important to know all those things you can offer to people you will be meeting. By completing this questionnaire, you will have—all in one place—everything you can share every time you meet someone new.

- Write down your areas of knowledge and expertise (things you know well).

_____

_____

_____

- Make a list of key people you know and you have access to.

_____

_____

_____

- Make a list of inside information you have access to (it could be when the new fall collection will hit the stores where you work, which gives shoppers a heads up; or you might know about openings in your company).

_____

_____

_____

- Make a list of organizations that you have access to (professional organizations, clubs, etc.).

- Make a list of things you have access to (it could be financial capital, free meeting space, etc.).

All the items you just listed are things you have to offer when you network. The people you meet might want access to money you can get, need your connection to the director of the diversity department of your company, or want to talk to you because you know several professionals in various fields who are bilingual and who are great assets if a company is looking for them. This is your capital, and you need to constantly develop it and preserve it. What this means is that you have to feed your capital as much as you feed your network. You should not take anybody or anything for granted.

Latinos have a natural charm and sociability that makes them great candidates to succeed at networking. They understand the power of an extended group

CAREER TIP

Employee Referral Programs (ERPs), programs through which current employees can refer people they know for open positions, have become a major source of candidates for companies and a good way to earn extra money for employees (they almost always carry a monetary reward). The reason is simple— employees who come through these programs normally assimilate better, since they have insight into the company's culture before they join, provided by those who are referring them. Also, as someone who refers others, you will have many grateful people who will be willing to help out when you need it.

of people looking out for them. To network effectively, you need to prepare and put in the effort it requires. Do not underestimate the level of professionalism you need to apply to this activity in order to succeed. Always be prepared and never take it personally. Do not take your network for granted—feed it frequently. Be aware of what you have to offer. You will only learn networking by practicing, and the more you practice, the better you will get at it.

PROFILE
Lillian Ortiz—Equal Access Warrior

Lillian Ortiz is a lawyer and the vice president of the Hispanic National Bar Association. That description, however, does not do her trajectory any justice. Although her difficult beginnings are similar to what many Latinos have endured in order to achieve the American Dream, the truth is that Lillian has lived and continues to live quite an unusual life.

Her parents, who had little education and were very poor, came from Puerto Rico in search of a better life. Her father worked many hours and tried different jobs until he found a profession in metal design. Through hard work and sacrifice, their situation improved and Lillian had the opportunity to attend Catholic school, first in the Bronx and later on Long Island.

"This is the land of opportunity, and education is the key that can open all those doors," explains Lillian, who studied International Affairs at the University of Colorado. She understood early on the power of education as the vehicle to achieving her dreams, given the opportunities that school networks open for alumni. She believes many Latinos do not quite appreciate the important role education plays in opening doors.

International Affairs was only Lillian's first career. A BA in Education followed, then a Masters in Spanish, and finally a law degree when she was fifty years old and had already raised two children. Law became her passion and the area where she focuses the most today. Given that less than 2% of all law students are Latinos, Lillian is concerned about the composition of the judicial system. "No Latino lawyers means no Latino judges; and with the large proportion of minorities that go through the criminal and judicial system, it is very important to get lawyers and judges who understand the multiple cultural baggage."

Law is far from being Lillian's only focus. She never stops learning and then sharing what she learns with others by participating in different forums and even in politics. (Lillian was appointed to the office of Latino Affairs in the governorship of Ohio.) She also speaks several languages, a point she strongly emphasizes. "Language has an economic value, but in order to extract that value you have to be proficient at it, and I mean both languages: English and Spanish, spoken and written."

She believes that Latinos feel very comfortable in their immediate network. "It's a false sense of comfort," Lillian says. So, she encourages Latinos to reach out of that close-knit network and learn from others. When asked about which areas Latinos should improve, Lillian places networking first and mentoring right next to it. She admits that much of her success is due to these two valuable skills. "Americans are absolute experts at this. They understand the concept of mentoring and how powerful it could be as a developmental tool." Lillian takes advantage of mentoring every day to connect people with each other and to continue to advance in her own career.

When asked about the most important attributes for Latinos to succeed in America, Lillian does not hesitate. "We have the right values (conservative) for this country and this is key; we have very strong role models in our families, most of whom have sacrificed a lot in order to come here." However, she also points out that it is very important for Latinos to learn how the system works in order to take better advantage of the available resources. "Latinos don't participate enough," she regrets, "and the only way to influence the system is through active involvement." According to Lillian, Latinos don't get organized as easily as other ethnic groups, missing out on the chance to further spread their influence in this country. The future is brilliant for Latinos as long as they continue to work on this very crucial point—as long as they learn to network with larger groups and associations that can help them advance in the American system.

It is obvious that Lillian owes her success in great part to her conviction that education opens doors and to her relentless networking. Meeting people who put her in touch with other people allowed her to always stay involved with issues that are relevant to her and to the Latino community.

PART 4

Bringing it All
TOGETHER

EPILOGUE

Numbers are not enough. We need a lot more in order to increase our influence in America. We need to keep improving ourselves and working hard to show how absolutely essential our values and skills are for the U.S. to continue to hold its premier position in the world.

Throughout this book, we have tried to give you varied tools that should help you improve your chances of success. How much you get out of it is a function of your level of commitment to living the Latino Advantage.

As we have said often, it will take hard work: reflection, practice, and above all, self-awareness. You should always keep in mind that all the advantages you have as a Latino could easily become short-comings if not managed properly.

We believe that the time for Latinos to claim their place in the sun is here. All the necessary conditions have been met and America is ready to appreciate all the value we can add. Now you have to do your part.

To wrap up the ideas introduced in these pages, let's go over the main lessons we think you should take with you:

❏ Build self-awareness.
  ■ Know your innate traits well so you can manage them effectively.
  ■ Remember how important the image you project is to your success.
  ■ Ask for feedback often, whether it is from your boss, your colleagues or your friends. Keep in mind that perceptions become reality for those who have them.

❏ Create your own image.
  ■ Learn to identify stereotypes and fight them successfully. Denying your origins is not the way to do it.
  ■ Show your individuality.

❏ Use your diverse background in a positive way.
  ■ Remember that companies are fighting for that unique idea that will give them the edge, and that your diverse background could be the key.
  ■ Always learn the more and less positive aspects of your cultural background.
  ■ Achieve balance.
  ■ Be yourself. Know the richness of your heritage.

❏ Build bridges with other minority groups and nonminority groups.
  ■ Learn from them. Just as Latinos have their advantages and shortcomings, so do all cultures.

❏ Teach others.
  ■ It is your responsibility to teach other fellow Latinos and non-Latinos what you have learned, such as the power of diverse perspectives and the importance of self-awareness.

❑ Never stop learning.
- The only way to succeed is to keep an edge on others; and the key to maintaining your edge is learning new tricks.

❑ Set clear goals for yourself and your career.
- Goals should be specific, realistic, and on a timeline.
- Review your goals often to make sure they still reflect your motivation, desires, and the context you are in.

DIRECTORY OF RESOURCES

As you begin to implement many of the ideas we shared in this book, you may find yourself looking for resources that will support your growth. We have compiled a list of some very useful resources that you may want to explore. It includes both private and governmental organizations, job portals that are particularly good for Latinos, and professional associations, as well as books that will help you in a variety of areas.

Please beware that with the constant changes taking place on the Internet, some of these websites will change address or design by the time you read this book. If you have difficulty finding a site, type the name of the organization or company in the search engine of your choice. That should take you to the correct address.

EMPLOYMENT RESOURCES

American Staffing Association (ASA)
277 South Washington Street
Suite 200
Alexandria, VA 22314
703-253-2020
Fax: 703-253-2053
www.americanstaffing.com

A nonprofit organization that promotes the interest of its members, staffing companies. Their website allows you to search by state and then choose agencies that specialize in your profession or occupation.

CareerOneStop
www.careeronestop.org
877-348-0502

A collection of tools operating as a federal-state partnership and funded by grants to states. Each tool offers a unique solution from the perspective of the job seeker, the employer, and the public workforce community. It includes three separate career resource tools: 1) *America's Job Bank* allows you to search through a database of over one million jobs nationwide, create and post your résumé online, and set up an automated job search. The database contains a wide range of mostly full-time private sector jobs that are available all over the country. Visit them at **www.ajb.org**. 2) *America's Career InfoNet* provides information on educational, licensing, and certification requirements for different occupations by state. It also provides information on wages, cost of living, and employment trends, and helps job seekers identify their skills, and write résumés and cover letters. Visit their website at **www.acinet.org**. 3) *America's Service Locator* provides listings of local employment service offices that help jobseekers find jobs and help employers find qualified workers at no cost to either.

Hispanic Alliance for Career Advancement (HACE)
25 East Washington
Suite 820
Chicago, IL 60602
312-435-0498
Fax: 312-435-1494
www.hace-usa.org

An organization that specializes in helping Latinos develop careers. You can post your résumé and search the database for job offerings.

League of United Latin American Citizens (LULAC)
2000 L Street, NW
Suite 610
Washington, DC 20036
202-833-6130
www.lulac.org

Offers employment and training programs, conducts research, and encourages voter registration. They have a large number of links to private and government organizations, media, Latino sites and portals, policy centers, etc.

National Association of Personnel Services (NAPS)
P.O. Box 2128
Banner Elk, NC 28604
828-898-4929
www.recruitinglife.com

The organization that certifies recruiting professionals nationwide. They have a directory online that lists employment agencies of all types by occupational specialization and by geographical coverage.

National Association of Workforce Boards
4350 North Fairfax Drive
Suite 220
Arlington, VA 22203
www.nawb.org (click member directory to find your state)
703-778-7900 ext. 111 (for information on your local chapter)

This organization represents business-led workforce boards that plan and oversee state and local workforce development and job training programs like One Stop Centers. These centers specialize in helping people overcome any barriers they might have to employment. They provide training on a wide range of topics, as well as counseling and referrals.

POWERFUL HISPANIC ASSOCIATIONS

Hispanic Association on Corporate Responsibility (HACR)
1444 I Street, NW
Suite 850
Washington, DC 20005
202-835-9672
Fax: 202-457-0455
www.hacr.org

A nonprofit organization whose mission is to lead the inclusion of Hispanics in corporate America at a level commensurate with their economic contributions.

National Society of Hispanic Professionals (NSHP)
1835 Northeast Miami Gardens Drive
#313
North Miami Beach, FL 33179
www.nshp.org

A nonprofit organization whose mission is to empower Hispanic professionals with information and connections. Its purpose is to provide Hispanic professionals with networking and leadership opportunities, as well as information on education, careers, and entrepreneurship.

League of United Latin American Citizens (LULAC)
2000 L Street, NW
Suite 610
Washington, DC 20036
202-833-6130
Fax: 202-833-6135
www.lulac.org

A nonprofit organization whose mission is to advance the economic condition, educational attainment, political influence, health, and civil rights of the Hispanic population of the United States.

National Association of Latino Elected and Appointed Officials (NALEO)
1122 West Washington Boulevard
Los Angeles, CA 90015
213-747-7606
Fax: 213-747-7664
www.naleo.org

A nonpartisan 501(c)(4) organization whose constituency is comprised by the more than six thousand elected and appointed Latino officials.

National Council of La Raza (NCLR)
Raul Yzaguirre Building
1126 16th Street, NW
Washington, DC 20036
202-785-1670
www.nclr.org

The largest civil rights and advocacy organization in the United States. Together with its affiliates, it conducts research in regards to Hispanics.

National Hispanic Corporate Council (NHCC)
1530 Wilson Boulevard
Suite 110
Arlington, VA 22209
703-807-5137
Fax: 703-842-7924
www.nhcc-hq.org

A nonprofit organization seeking to provide a clearinghouse of Hispanic marketing information, expertise, and counsel for companies.

National Hispanic Employee Association (MENTóR)
25A Crescent Drive
#312
Pleasant Hill, CA 94523
202-842-4812
www.mentores.org

A nonprofit organization that provides training, mentoring, and networking opportunities.

New America Alliance
6688 North Central Expressway
Suite 625
Dallas, TX 75206
214-466-6410
Fax: 214-466-6415
www.naaonline.org

An organization of American Latino business leaders united to promote the advancement of the American Latino community.

SER—Jobs for Progress National, Inc.
5215 North O'Connor Boulevard
Suite 2550
Irving, TX 75039
972-506-7815
Fax: 972-506-7832
www.ser-national.org

A nonprofit corporation with special emphasis in addressing the needs of Hispanics in the areas of education, job skill training, literacy, and employment opportunities. The website has comprehensive job listing.

JOB PORTALS (INTERNET)

Bilingual Jobs: **www.bilingual-jobs.com**

A website designed for people fluent in English who are also fluent in another language.

Careers.org: **www.careers.org**

A wonderful site where you will find an entire list of valuable websites to help you in your career search. It has links to websites that list jobs by state, professional area, diversity, and many more categories. Do not miss this one!

CVlatino: **www.cvlatino.com**

You can post your résumé, search for jobs, and find a good list of Latino websites.

Diversity Inc: **www.diversityinc.com**

This website publishes *Diversity* magazine, a paid circulation magazine featuring articles related to diversity in the workforce. With the subscription, you also have access to a list of the top companies hiring minorities.

Ihispano.com: **www.ihispano.com**

A job site specialized in jobs targeted for Latinos.

Imdiversity.com: **www.imdiversity.com**

A job site specialized in listings for minorities.

Joblatino: **www.joblatino.com**

A site where you can post your résumé and search for jobs. It also offers useful tips and links to Latino organizations.

Latpro: **www.latpro.com**

This website specializes in jobs for the Latino professional. Post your résumé and search for jobs across the country. You can also subscribe to their email service to receive jobs that match what you are looking for.

Saludos.com: **www.saludos.com**

This website features a list of jobs and top-ranking companies that hire Latinos.

PROFESSIONAL ASSOCIATIONS AND RESOURCES

The Association of Latino Professionals in Finance and Accounting (ALPFA)
801 South Grand Avenue
Suite 400
Los Angeles, CA 90017
213-243-0004
Fax: 213-243-0006
www.alpfa.org

A professional nonprofit association dedicated to enhancing opportunities for Latinos in the accounting, finance, and related professions.

Hispanic Alliance for Career Enhancement (HACE)
25 East Washington Street
Suite 820
Chicago, IL 60602
312-435-0498
Fax: 312-435-1494
www.hace-usa.org

An organization that specializes in helping Latinos develop careers. You can post your job and search their database for job offerings.

Hispanic National Bar Associaiton (HNBA)
815 Connecticut Avenue, NW
Suite 500
Washington, DC 20006
202-223-4777
Fax: 202-223-2324
www.hnba.com

A nonprofit, national association representing the interest of over 25,000 Hispanic American attorneys, judges, law professors, and law students in the United States and Puerto Rico.

Hispanic Nurses Association
1501 16th Street, NW
Washington, DC 20036
202 387-2477
Fax: 202-483-7183
www.thehispanicnurses.org

A nonprofit organization to promote Hispanic nurses to improve the health care of the Latino community. Organizes annual conference.

National Society of Hispanic MBAs (NSHMBA)
1303 Walnut Hill Lane
Suite 100
Irving, TX 75038
214-596-9338
Fax: 214-596-9325
www.nshmba.org

A nonprofit organization fostering Hispanic leadership through graduate management education and professional development in order to improve society.

National Association of Social Workers (NASW)
750 1st Street, NE
Suite 700
Washington, DC 20002
202-408-8600
www.naswdc.org

With 153,000 members, NASW works to enhance the professional growth and development of its members, to create and maintain professional standards, and to advance social policies. You can find information about conferences, jobs, credentialing, and much more on their website.

National Association of Hispanic Journalists (NAHJ)
1000 National Press Building
529 14th Street, NW
Washington, DC 20045
202-662-7145
Fax: 202-662-7144
www.nahj.org

Dedicated to the recognition and professional advancement of Hispanics in the news industry.

National Hispanic Medical Association (NHMA)
1411 K Street, NW
Suite 1000
Washington, DC 20005
202-628-5895
Fax: 202-628-5898
www.nhmamd.org

Provides policymakers and health care providers with expert information and support in strengthening health service delivery to Hispanic communities across the nation.

Society of Hispanic Professional Engineers (SHPE)
5400 East Olympic Boulevard
Suite 210
Los Angeles, CA 90022
323-725-3970
www.shpe.org

Promotes the development of Hispanics in engineering, science, and other technical professions to achieve educational excellence, economic opportunity, and social equity.

Society of Mexican American Engineers and Scientists (MAES)
711 West Bay Area Boulevard
Suite 206
Webster, TX 77598
281-557-3677
Fax: 281-557-3757
www.maes-natl.org

An organization with a national membership representing all the engineering and scientific disciplines of the Mexican-American community.

RESOURCES FOR LATINO BUSINESSES

Hispanic Business
425 Pine Avenue
Santa Barbara, CA 93117
805-964-4554
Fax: 805-964-5539
www.hispanicbusiness.com

A gateway to the Hispanic business community all over the U.S. with a collective brochure of all Latino entrepreneurs trying to do business with major corporations.

Hispanic Business Women's Alliance
The Atrium Center
530 Avenida de la Constitución
San Juan, Puerto Rico 00901
787-289-7843
www.hbwa.net

An online community that enables you to do business, share information and ideas, and collaborate with other Hispanic women in North America, Latin America, the Caribbean, and Spain.

Latin Business Association
120 South San Pedro Street
Suite 530
Los Angeles, CA 90012
213-628-8510
www.lbausa.com

A professional organization dedicated to the success of Hispanic businesses.

United States Hispanic Chamber of Commerce (USHCC)
2175 K Street, NW
Suite 100
Washington, DC 20037
800-USHCC86
202-842-1212
Fax: 202-842-3221
www.ushcc.com

An organization working towards bringing the issues and concerns of the nation's more than one million Hispanic-owned businesses to the forefront of the national economic agenda. The site enables you to find chambers of commerce by state.

United States-Mexico Chamber of Commerce (USMCOC)
Binational Headquarters
1300 Pennsylvania Avenue, NW
Suite G-0003
Washington, DC 20004
202-312-1520
Fax: 202-312-1530
www.usmcoc.org

A nonprofit corporation and a chartered binational organization promoting trade and investment between the two American nations. The Chamber represents more than one thousand businesses in the United States and Mexico.

The Women's Business Centers
Office of Women's Business Ownership
Small Business Administration
409 3rd Street, SW
6th Floor
Washington, DC 20416
202-205-6673
www.onlinewbc.gov

Represent a national network of more than one hundred educational centers designed to assist women to start and grow small companies. Their goal is to help women achieve self sufficiency through economic independence. They offer a whole range of training courses to teach women how to start up and run a business. Visit their website to find out programs near you targeted at Latinas.

SCHOLARSHIPS FOR LATINOS

Hispanic Scholarship Fund
55 2nd Street
Suite 1500
San Francisco, CA 94105
877-HSF-INFO (877-473-4636)
Fax: 415-808-2302
www.hsf.net

The Hispanic Scholarship Fund (HSF) is the nation's leading organization supporting Hispanic higher education. HSF was founded in 1975 with a vision to strengthen the country by advancing college education among Hispanic Americans—the largest minority segment of the U.S. population. In support of its mission to double the rate of Hispanics earning college degrees, HSF provides the Latino community more college scholarships and educational outreach support than any other organization in the country. It distributed twenty-five million in scholarships to Latinos in 2005–2006.

Hispanic College Fund
1717 Pennsylvania Avenue, NW
Suite 460
Washington, DC 20006
800-644-4223
www.hispanicfund.org

The Hispanic College Fund's mission is to educate and develop the next generation of Hispanic professionals. Their scholarship programs focus on developing Latino youth who are pursuing undergraduate degrees in business, science, engineering, technology, and math.

They award merit- and need-based scholarships to Latino students and providing them with vision, resources, tools, and mentors so that they can achieve their full potential as professionals and leaders. In 2006, HCF awarded 550 scholarships, totaling $1.4 million.

Mexican American Legal Defense and Education Fund
(MALDEF)
1717 K Street NW
#311
Washington, DC 20036
202-293-2828
Fax: 202-293-2849
www.maldef.org

MALDEF is a national nonprofit organization whose mission is to protect and promote the civil rights of the more than forty million Latinos living in the United States. Making sure that there are no obstacles preventing this diverse community from realizing its dreams, MALDEF works to secure the rights of Latinos, primarily in the areas of employment, education, immigrants' rights, political access, and public resource equity.

On its website, you will find scholarships for Latino students who are undocumented.

RMHC/HACER Scholarship Program
Scholarship Program Administrators
P.O. Box 22376
Nashville, TN 37202
www.ronaldhouse.org/hacer2

A scholarship program sponsored by the Ronald McDonald House Charities, the McDonald's Corporation, and the local McDonald's Hispanic Owner/Operators Associations is specifically targeted to Latino high school seniors with an average 3.0 GPA who are residents of the U.S. Distributed around 1.6 million dollars in 2005–2006.

Gates Millennium Scholars
P.O. Box 10500
Fairfax, VA 22031
877-690-4677
www.gmsp.org

The Gates Millennium Scholars (GMS), funded by a grant from the Bill & Melinda Gates Foundation, was established in 1999 to provide outstanding African American, American Indian/Alaska Native, Asian Pacific Islander American, and Hispanic American students with an opportunity to complete an undergraduate college education in all discipline areas and a graduate education for those students pursuing studies in mathematics, science, engineering, education, library science, or public health. The scholarship offered by the Gates Foundation is administered through the United Negro College Fund, which partners with the Hispanic Scholarship Fund.

GENERAL ASSISTANCE

Centers for Disease Control—Office of Minority Health
Mailstop E-67
1600 Clifton Road, NE
Atlanta, GA 30333
404-498-2320
Fax: 404-498-2355
www.cdc.gov/omh

Features services provided by the U.S. Department of Health and Human Services that are of particular interest to the Hispanic community and organizations serving Hispanics.

Concilio Hispano
105 Windsor Street
Cambridge, MA 02139
617-661-9406
Fax: 617-661-8008
www.conciliohispano.org

A nonprofit organization that provides services to the greater Boston Latino community. They focus on fostering culture, self-identity, and advancement of Latinos and other minorities.

El Centro Hispano, Inc.
800 Allegheny Avenue
Suite 127
Pittsburgh, PA 15233
412-322-2716
Fax: 412-322-2718
www.pghhispaniccenter.org

A nonprofit corporation located in Pittsburgh with the mission to assist families who wish to successfully relocate to this region of southwestern Pennsylvania.

Hispanic Association of Colleges and Universities (HACU)
www.hnip.net

Represents more than three hundred colleges and universities committed to Hispanic higher education success in the U.S., Puerto Rico, Latin America, and Spain.

BOOKS AND PUBLICATIONS

The Americano Dream—ISBN #0452278317—By Lionel Sosa, published by Plume.

Published in 1999, it is still as current as it was then. Sosa intertwines his personal story with invaluable cultural observations that cover family life, business, and education.

Ayude a sus Hijos a Tener Éxito en la Escuela: Guía para Padres Latinos (Help your Children be Successful in School: Guide for Latino Parents)—ISBN #1572485477—By Mariela Dabbah, published by Sourcebooks.

A step-by-step guide for Latino parents to understand how the American education system works. From the logistics involved in school, to how to help your child develop academic skills with every day activities, to how to get involved in the school system when you don't have time, this book dispels myths and gives you the key to help your children succeed.

Best Careers for Bilingual Latinos—ISBN #0844245410—By Graciela Kenig, published by McGraw-Hill.

A wonderful resource about the top careers for bilingual Latinos.

Cómo Conseguir Trabajo en los Estados Unidos: Guía para Latinos (How to Get a Job in the U.S.: Guide for Latinos)—ISBN #1572484888—By Mariela Dabbah, published by Sourcebooks.

A practical guide, full of expert advice, written from the Latino perspective to find a job in the US. It covers available resources for job seekers, the best methods to find a job, techniques to write a winning resume, how to ace a job interview, and how to negotiate a job offer.

Cómo Escribir un Currículum Vitae en Inglés que Tenga Éxito—ISBN #0844272949—By Marcia Seidletz, published by McGraw-Hill.

This book is filled with examples of résumés for all sorts of occupations. The bilingual format (résumés are all listed in Spanish and English) helps readers transition from writing their own résumé in Spanish to translating it into English.

Fund Your Future: Winning Strategies for Managing Your Mutual Funds and 401(K)—ISBN #0425196054—By Julie Stav, published by Berkley Trade.

In this updated edition of *Fund Your Future*, Julie Stav, the host of a popular radio show on Univision radio, shows step-by-step how to set financial goals and examine your current investment plans to determine if you are investing as profitably as possible. Her signature blend of supportiveness and expert practical advice takes the fear out of investing and puts the roadmap to riches within easy reach.

Get Your Share: A Guide to Striking It Rich in the Stock Market—ISBN #0425193977—By Julie Stav, published by Berkley Trade.

This detailed guide to owning stocks and bonds is a must for anyone ready to move beyond passbook savings and CDs. It covers the principles of equity ownership in a way that assumes nothing of listeners. The book also explains a detailed system for analyzing the value of individual stocks, stock sectors, and the market in general. The subject matter is technical, but Julie Stav knows how to explain without talking down to her readers.

Job Search Guide for Latinos—ISBN #0764128698—By Murray Mann and Rose Mary Bombela-Tobias, published by Barron's.

This book presents a comprehensive career road map designed to resonate with Latino and Hispanic job seekers at experience levels ranging from college students through mid-level managers. If you area Latino job seeker, you will find user-friendly advice and information you can use right away.

Latino Success—ISBN #0684833425—by Augusto Failde and William Doyle, published by Fireside.

A greatly inspirational book with stories and advice from one hundred successful Latinos. It includes a list of one hundred best companies for Latinos. The book was published in 1997 but the information is valuable and still current.

Los 7 pasos para ser más feliz: Cómo Liberarte del Estrés, las Preocupaciones y las Angustias del Pasado (The 7 steps to Being Happier: How to Free Yourself from Stress, Worries and Anxieties from the Past)—ISBN #9780307276575—By Dr. Isabel Gomez-Bassols, published by Vintage.

Happiness is the world's most sought-after quality. In her newest book, Dr. Isabel, the host of a very popular radio show on Univision Radio, offers advice, exercises, and techniques to help you reach a higher level of happiness in your life.

The Money in You!: Discover Your Financial Personality and Live the Millionaire's Life—ISBN #0060854901—By Julie Stav, published by Rayo.

Julie Stav, the host of a popular radio show on Univision Radio, introduces us to five different financial personality types. According to Julie, it is our financial nature—the way we handle money matters—that forecasts our financial future. Julie shows readers that no amount of data or market expertise trumps the fundamental truth we all forget—that building wealth, attaining security, and establishing personal success can only be achieved when we recognize our strengths and weaknesses.

Think and Grow Rich: A Latino Choice—ISBN #0345485610—By Lionel Sosa with the Napoleon Hill Foundation, published by Ballantine Books.

The latest Lionel Sosa book shows how, applying the proven principles of preparation, competence, hard work, and sincerity devised by legendary motivational author Napoleon Hill, Sosa advanced from painting signs at $1.10 an hour to running the largest Hispanic ad agency in America. In this guide to prosperity, Sosa shares his inspiring story of achievement, as well as those of other respected members of the Latino community.

When I Say No, I Feel Guilty—ISBN #0553263900—by Manuel J. Smith, published by Bantam; reissue edition.

A great book with practical advice for asserting yourself when you need to.

LET'S PRACTICE

The objective of these activities is to help you reflect upon your origins and some of the advantages (and disadvantages) you already have as a result of your heritage. Many of these are things you do without thinking much—ways of approaching an issue, resolving a problem, interacting with people, and so on. Analyzing them and breaking them down into smaller pieces will help you understand what you are doing and how you are doing it. It will be a bit hard at first, but after a few activities, you will be able to extract the generic skills that your Latino upbringing has given you and apply them to different settings.

MAXIMIZING OPPORTUNITIES

To increase your awareness regarding the impact of your cultural background in your workplace, start with a simple activity.

- List a few instances when your Latino background helped you in any way (e.g., someone shared important information with you, you got a better assignment at work, etc.).

_____

_____

_____

_____

- Why do you think this happened?

_____

_____

_____

_____

Now think of the opposite situation.

- List a few instances when your Latino background hindered your progress at work in any way (e.g., people made assumptions about your behavior or your abilities, etc.).

_____

_____

_____

_____

- Why do you think this happened? (Try to think of things you actively did. If you were the object of a discriminatory action, reflect on that as well.)

_____

_____

_____

_____

USING YOUR LANGUAGE

If you have not experienced language as a tool to establish relationships yet, try any of the following. Write about what happens in each situation on the lines provided.

- At a restaurant, when you notice that the waiter or the host speaks Spanish, order in Spanish. If you cannot, at least say "Hola, ¿cómo está?" If you are the waiter and you notice that a guest speaks Spanish, welcome him or her in that language.

_____

_____

_____

_____

_____

- At your childs school, when you notice that an administrative person speaks Spanish, talk to him or her in Spanish.

_____

_____

_____

_____

_____

- If you meet someone you like and he or she has a Latino background, say a few words in Spanish and observe the reaction.

_____

_____

_____

_____

_____

When you use your language skills even in these causal ways, you will see a spark in the eyes of those you talk to, and you most likely will feel a connection that will translate into better service, a bigger tip, and all kinds of opportunities.

STEREOTYPES AND THE BATTLE FOR BALANCE

List a situation in which you made a big effort to move away from your own Latino heritage (it could be to avoid a stereotype). For example, you may have denied your origin by not telling anyone at work that you could speak or understand Spanish, decided not to join a Hispanic network in your company, or made negative comments about Latinos to your colleagues to make sure nobody would associate you with them.

■ What was the situation?

_____

_____

_____

_____

■ What did you do?

_____

_____

_____

_____

■ What was the stereotype (lateness, unreliability, etc.)?

_____

_____

_____

_____

■ What was the explanation you gave yourself as a justification for your actions?

_____

_____

_____

_____

■ What was the outcome?

_____

_____

_____

_____

Now, try to think of the same situation and consider ways in which you could embrace your culture, maximize the advantages it can bring to the workplace, and still be part of the American culture.

■ What would you do differently?

_____

_____

_____

_____

■ What edge would that approach give you?

_____

_____

_____

_____

■ How can you turn the situation around now? (For example, if in the past you decided not to join the Hispanic network in the office, you can join it now.)

_____

_____

_____

_____

THE IMPORTANCE OF FAMILY

Think about an important party that you organized for your family. It can be a quinceañera or a wedding—it does not matter. Try to recall all the people you invited, plus the people you talked to in order to make it happen. You probably spoke to lots of individuals you know well to help you coordinate the food, music, decorations, clothing, location, and so on.

■ Make a list of all the activities that were involved.

_____

_____

_____

■ List any obstacles you had to overcome during the organization of this event (for example, having to invite members of the family that do not particularly get along and decide how to sit them) and how you worked with your network to overcome those obstacles.

_____

_____

_____

Now think for a moment about your job. Pretend that you have to organize an event (a conference or a party for other employees or for customers). Do you have the contacts you need to pull off a successful event? The skills you need to produce a successful event at work are the same you use at home to pull off a successful party.

■ Do you notice that sometimes when it comes to establishing relationships you behave differently at work than at home? (For instance, you are shy to approach new people.) What are some of those differences?

_____

_____

_____

HONESTY

Write down a situation in which your internal values conflicted with a particular rule or law and how you dealt with the situation. The goal of this exercise is to reflect on the good intentions you might have had (or will have in the future) in instances such as this one, and the impact of your actions. There will be plenty of gray areas in which the right answer will be difficult to find; but it is critical to understand how people with different values and cultural backgrounds would perceive these actions.

Use the following example as a guide.

- Situation: My coworker is stealing expensive office supplies.
- Your action: I do not report her.
- Your perspective: I privilege our friendship over a rule.
- Alternate perspective: These supplies are for the office, so it hurts me too to have them stolen. I'll report her to the boss.
- Impact of your action: I'm reinforcing my friend's wrong behavior and hurting the office as a whole.
- Other possible reactions and effects: I talk to my coworker to explain the impact of her behavior and warn her that this is the last time I will keep quiet.

- Situation:

_____

_____

_____

_____

- Your action:

_____

_____

_____

_____

■ Your perspective:

_____

_____

_____

_____

■ Alternate perspective:

_____

_____

_____

_____

■ Impact of your action:

_____

_____

_____

_____

■ Other possible reactions and effects:

_____

_____

_____

_____

_____

_____

_____

_____

Remember, what the world sees is not the intention of your actions, but their impact. Think about what your intention was when you behaved that way. Think about what the impact of your behavior was. Finally, try to put yourself in an American's shoes and think about how they would have reacted in the same situation.

GOAL SETTING

Think about the first generation of your family that came to America—those special people who broke new ground or achieved new objectives. Try to visualize them. Put yourself in their shoes. If you are not that familiar with the details, do some research on it. If you are that person, then you will have to go back to your own thoughts and objectives when you started planning to come over to America.

The objective of this exercise is to reconstruct a success story. Yes, leaving your home country and starting a new life is in itself a success story. You set a goal and you achieved it. In all likelihood, when you look into your family's history (or into your own), you will find that the key to success is to structure your efforts in an efficient way.

Once you have your family story, answer the following questions.

■ What were the goals they/you set out to achieve?

_____

_____

_____

_____

_____

_____

■ How did they/you go about organizing themselves/yourself to achieve those goals?

_____

_____

_____

_____

_____

_____

- What short-term sacrifices did they/you make in order to obtain longer-term goals?

_____

_____

_____

_____

_____

_____

- Set out a chronology of events.

_____

_____

_____

_____

_____

- Consider other questions you think may be valuable to ask. (For example, how did they advance in their careers? Did they find mentors along the way?)

_____

_____

_____

_____

_____

Use this exercise as a practice on how to set small goals for yourself and on how to organize your actions towards those goals.

RESPECT FOR AUTHORITY

Think of a situation where your upbringing conflicted with the way things are done in America. For example, you may address your boss more formally or greet people at a company party by kissing them on the cheek, like many Latinos are used to. Now think about how these same things are done here and consider the critical difference. How does that difference impact you?

Being overly formal might delay creating a productive relationship with your boss or make you feel less comfortable to express your ideas with him or her. At the company party, touching others when you talk, or kissing them, might make people uncomfortable or feel that you are invading their space.

- How would you approach these different situations now? List your strategies and action plan.

_____

_____

_____

_____

_____

_____

_____

_____

_____

_____

_____

_____

THE NEED TO PLEASE

Think of at least three situations in which, looking back, you should have said no or given bad news up front.

■ What was the situation?

_____

_____

_____

■ What was your intention when you said yes or set the expectations higher than you thought were realistic?

_____

_____

_____

■ What was the impact? (Was the other person disappointed, upset, etc.?)

_____

_____

_____

■ Looking back, what would you have done differently? (Even if you understand the negative impact that comes with not saying no, some situations are very difficult to confront. It will become easier immediately, but you have to start practicing.)

_____

_____

_____

Spend this week observing how you and other Latinos around you avoid saying no when it would be appropriate or wise to do so.

During the next few days, practice saying no to simple requests even if you could actually fulfill them. For instance, a colleague asks if you could cover the phones over lunchtime. Say something like, "I'm sorry. I have a commitment at lunchtime. I won't be able to."

DON'T TAKE IT PERSONALLY

Think of an instance in which you allowed your emotions to take over during what should have been just a business transaction. (For example, you asked for a colleague to review your work and give you feedback, but then got very upset when he or she gave you the comments back.)

■ What was the situation?

_____

_____

■ What made you cross the line and take it personally? (Did you feel it was a personal attack? Was the language too direct?)

_____

_____

■ What opportunity was lost because of this shift to the personal level? (Did you miss some comments that could have improved the quality of your work?)

_____

_____

■ Looking back, what could you have done differently? (For example, if someone gives you feedback using harsh language, you can tell him or her how you feel, or you can ask a third party to review the comments and assess their validity if you feel you are too close to the issue to make an impartial assessment.)

_____

_____

It is important that you reflect on these situations and understand clearly the impact of your actions. Always keep in mind that with stereotypes, many people are waiting to confirm their perceptions and even their prejudices. Using other people as role models will help you see the situation from a different perspective.

ADAPTABILITY

The objective of this activity is to reflect on situations that you or your family have faced in the past. You will see how the strategies you used to cope with these situations can be easily applied to experiences encountered at work.

- Write down a life example that involved change for you or your family. (For instance, the last economic crisis, which forced some of your family members to move to the U.S. to live with you.)

_____

_____

_____

_____

_____

_____

- List the actions taken to adjust to this change.

_____

_____

_____

_____

_____

_____

- To what extent are these actions similar (and applicable) to the latest big change in the workplace (reorganization, job transition, etc.) that you or someone you know have gone through?

_____

_____

_____

_____

_____

_____

EXTREME ADAPTABILITY

Sometimes your adaptability trait has become so entrenched that you cannot distinguish good from bad anymore. Use a friend, former boss, or mentor as a sounding board to uncover situations in which you are being taken advantage of because of your nice demeanor. For example, perhaps you are asked to stay late at work more often than anyone else.

Once you have done this, and you have identified which battle you want to fight, planning is your best strategy. It is important to prepare a script of what you want to say to your supervisor and that you practice it before having a meeting to discuss the issues. No topic is off-limits as long as you present it carefully and respectfully. Keep in mind that the longer you wait to speak up about issues that are bothering you, the more difficult it will be to keep your emotions under control.

CREATIVITY

The objective of this exercise is to analyze and learn from alternative ways of dealing with different sorts of challenges. (If you have lived all your life in the U.S., you should ask your parents and grandparents to help you with this activity.)

■ Think of something you take for granted in the U.S. (For example, using the mail to pay your bills or even having a telephone line at home.) Now think of that same process in your heritage country (or ask your family how they did it).

■ List the differences and pay close attention to the creative ways they had to come up with in order to overcome the failure of the infrastructure or the scarcity of the resources. (For example, they used the phone at the pharmacy nearby, or the banks invented automatic debit in order to pay bills securely.)

_____

_____

If you cannot think of any examples, reflect on one of these:
■ Complex bureaucracies
■ Inadequate mail or phone service
■ Unsafe taxi cabs
■ Regular blackouts
■ No air conditioning
■ Unstable banking systems
■ Work-related

Now think of work related situations or challenges that you have faced lately. Try to use some of the same approaches to address them. If you work for a small company (or a start-up), you are very familiar with resources being scarce. On the other hand, if you work for a big company, you most likely face long, bureaucratic processes that reduce efficiency. Do you see any connection with the types of problems or challenges described above?

ACTIVATING YOUR CREATIVE SELF

Think about this: how could you apply your creativity to the American system? To get you started, here are two examples of things that were invented in Latin America due to scarcity of infrastructure or resources.

■ Given the inefficiency of the mail service, people usually paid their bills in person at the corresponding utility company. For this reason, automatic debit (from a checking account or credit card) came into existence much earlier in Latin America than in the U.S. It was a safer and more efficient way to pay.

■ Due to high gasoline prices, companies came up with fuel alternatives years before that became an issue for Americans. Cars that run on diesel and natural gas are a common occurrence in Latin America.

Now consider some ways you can apply your creative thinking to challenging situations in your workplace. Remember, just thinking *there has to be another way* can trigger creative ways to resolve challenging situations.

_____

_____

_____

_____

_____

_____

_____

_____

_____

_____

_____

_____

INDIRECTNESS

- Write down a situation at work when you used your indirect communication style and it had a negative effect. (For example, you did not openly refuse to take on an assignment that you knew you could not fulfill because you did not have the required tools.)

_____

_____

_____

- Why did your style elicit a negative effect? Did your actions show you as an uncommitted employee, untrustworthy, or lacking backbone? Try to put your finger on how your colleagues or bosses perceived you, and write it down.

_____

_____

_____

- How might a non-Latino friend have behaved in the same situation? What would he or she have done differently? (For example, he or she may have stated politely but firmly that he or she could not take on that assignment.)

_____

_____

_____

- Compare the two styles and note the differences. Appreciate why the more direct style would have elicited a more positive response in the same situation.

_____

_____

_____

Next time a similar situation arises, try your non-Latino friend's style.

HUMILITY

In career-related situations (job interview, networking, résumé, etc.) it is important for you to talk about your accomplishments in a way that lets others know exactly what they are. The best way to become good at this is by practicing with friends and then trying the technique in your work environment. The following exercise will help you take the first step.

Choose a friend and invite him or her for coffee. Explain that you need to practice talking about yourself in professional situations. Then spend ten minutes telling him or her what you have accomplished in your career up to now. You can also talk about your accomplishments in your life if you have not been working for a while. Make sure that you refer to yourself as "I" and not as "we," and that you only talk about your own personal achievements.

When you finish, ask your friend to describe your career-related achievements for you. Hearing someone else give you this feedback will reinforce your awareness of all you have accomplished. Then, ask your friend to tell you things you have accomplished that you may have left out.

JUSTIFYING MISTAKES

Realizing that you are justifying your mistakes is the key to changing your communication style to a more direct one where you can readily admit what went wrong and assume responsibility when appropriate. In this exercise, you will review your past experiences in dealing with mistakes and contrast them with your newly acquired knowledge.

Think about a recent mistake you have made in the workplace. (For example, you placed the wrong order and have to pay to return the goods.)

■ How did you handle the mistake? (Did you admit to it? Did you try to hide it from your boss or make up an excuse?)

_____
_____
_____
_____
_____
_____
_____

■ How would you have handled it now that you know how poorly it reflects on you to make excuses?

_____
_____
_____
_____
_____
_____
_____

Remain vigilant, and next time you make a mistake remember to avoid justifying it.

OFFERING EXCESSIVE CONTEXT

The first step towards becoming a better communicator is to be a good listener. In the following exercise, you will practice listening to your colleagues at work to try to mimic their style.

During the next two days, listen carefully to the way your American colleagues answer questions from their bosses or peers.

■ Take notes on what their answers are, and how long it takes them to answer.

_____

_____

_____

■ Now write down the ways in which you would have answered the same questions, and how long it probably would have taken you to answer.

_____

_____

_____

■ Compare both answers. Are they equivalent? What is different?

_____

_____

_____

Now pay attention to the questions people ask you in the office. Figure out what they really want to know and try to answer in a very concise way.

It will be awkward in the beginning, but as you become accustomed to responding in a less emotional and lengthy way, you will improve your opportunities of success in the American workplace.

INFORMALITY

In order for you to become more formal at work, you need to start observing your own behavior and practicing in small areas. The following exercise will walk you through the process.

- Write down a list of areas where you can identify yourself as being too informal (for example, the way in which you present your proposals to your supervisor or the way in which you set up meetings with your team).

_____

_____

_____

_____

- Choose one to work on first. Write down the steps you will follow to increase the level of formality with which you approach that area or task. (For example, call people beforehand even if there is a slight chance you will be late to a meeting or party, or type your proposals on your computer and hand them over in a folder.)

_____

_____

_____

_____

- Practice it for two or three days and write your observations. Can you see any changes in the way others respond to you when you behave more formally? As you become more formal in this area, you can then go down the list.

_____

_____

_____

_____

CONFLICT AVERSE VS. UNRELIABLE

Overcoming your conflict avoidance instincts will take some effort on your part. Use this exercise to reflect on some past situations when you did not speak up and to imagine different outcomes had you done so.

- Think of three examples of situations in which you had a different opinion than someone else at work and you did not say anything. Reflect on the situation. (For example, maybe a coworker suggested an idea you are sure will not work.)

_____

_____

- What was the rational explanation you gave yourself for your behavior? (Maybe the coworker has been there longer than you, so you reason he or she knows better than you.)

_____

_____

- If you had spoken your mind, what could have gone differently? (You might have been able to save the company time and money by respectfully pointing out the flaws in your coworker's suggestion.)

_____

_____

- Think of three actions you will take next time. Remember, we are not talking about arguing, fighting, or even an open confrontation (although those things might be necessary at times). This is just about acquiring a certain degree of comfort with the tension associated with a potential conflict; enough comfort to be able to express your views in a clear and orderly manner.

_____

_____

LEADERSHIP AND CONFLICT

Whether you grew up in Latin America or were raised by Latino parents, you are likely to carry around many contradictions. Words of encouragement to get out there and *show them who you are* mixed with *you had better keep quiet* have been instilled in you simultaneously. The point of this exercise is to reflect on some of those contradictions, many of which you are not even conscious of possessing.

Think of situations you remember that illustrate your Latino tendency to take secondary roles (like the one on page 75). It is possible that the more removed you are from your Latino roots, the more difficulty you will have to come up with an example. Some of the specific things to think about include the following.

- What was the message given to you by your parents about how to behave in America? Did they encourage you to take risks, or to try not to make waves and just fit in? Did they encourage you to volunteer to lead school projects or clubs, or let others lead?

_____

_____

- What were the reasons given to you for trying to persuade you in that direction? Did they say that your turn would come, or it was not that important to lead?

_____

_____

- Did you see a difference between what your parents taught you and what your parents' friends taught them? Think about the impact some of these messages have had in your career. Consider volunteering for the next project at work, or even approaching your boss about taking on more responsibility.

_____

_____

CONFLICT MANAGEMENT AND COMMUNICATION

When you are faced with stressful situations in your job, it is easy to hide behind your less assertive communication style to avoid conflict. Use this exercise to reflect on instances in which your communication style got in the way of getting something that you wanted or needed. It could be when you wanted something—a salary increase, a project, etc.—and instead of asking for it directly, you gave indirect signals, or when you had a good idea but you were not able to convey it effectively.

■ Write down one of those situations.

_____

_____

■ How did you craft the message? (How did you express your interest, your idea, or your desire?)

_____

_____

_____

■ What was the outcome?

_____

_____

_____

■ What do you think went wrong?

_____

_____

_____

■ How could you employ the three Ps next time to get the outcome you desire?

_____

_____

_____

NETWORKING

Before looking at what networking entails, a simple exercise to help identify the differences between networking among Latinos and networking among Americans is in order.

■ Write down the people you consider contacts. Do not just write the names, but also their occupation or relationship with you. (For example: Marta Juárez, cousin.)

_____

_____

Ask an American friend or colleague who has a substantial network to do the same. Compare the number of people on your lists.

Analyze the following:

■ What type of people did your friend consider contacts that you did not?

_____

_____

■ What was your rationale for not including those people on your list?

_____

_____

■ Look again at your list of contacts and that of your American friend or colleague. Can you think of people in different categories that you could network with? (For example, professionals you see regularly like your doctor, your accountant, people in industry associations, etc.) Write them down.

_____

_____

Now answer these questions and continue to add more people to your list.

- If you have children, could you network with the parents of their friends?

  _____

  _____

- If you attend church or temple, could you network with the other parishioners? What about the priest or rabbi?

  _____

  _____

- If you volunteer, could you network with the other volunteers in the organization?

  _____

  _____

- If you went to school or took courses in the past, can you contact old peers or professors?

  _____

  _____

- If you belong to any particular committee, could you network with the other members?

  _____

  _____

You now have a much more significant networking pool from which to work.

BASIC RULES OF NETWORKING

Prepare yourself to talk to people about you in an interesting and appealing way. What you say to people you meet for the first time will probably vary depending on the stage of your life and your career. Adjust your presentation to your circumstances.

Think about the main aspects that define who you are, what you know, where you have been, and what you bring in terms of value. Do not focus only on your professional side—think of your hobbies, interests, and anything that says something about you that can help you make a connection with someone else. Remember that networking means making friends and connecting at a human level with someone.

Prepare different versions of your presentation to be used in different situations—a shorter one (usually known as the *elevator speech*) that you should be able to cover in one to three minutes, and another, more detailed, one that can be more flexible. You can type this speech on a card to hand out when you are networking for a new job.

An example of an elevator speech that you would use if you were looking for a job follows.

"I am a medical secretary with four years' experience in an MD's office. I am proficient in Microsoft Word, Excel, PowerPoint, Access, and Outlook. Most recently I worked for Doctor Ricardo Pereyra's dental office in Mexico City, Mexico, where I was noted for exceptional phone skills and for handling pressure calmly. I have received bonuses for my contribution to office efficiency. I have learned that I have the professional skills to work as a personal assistant. I am bilingual."

Following is a speech you would use if you were just socializing at an event, trying to meet new people to add to your network.

"I live in New York. I'm a medical secretary at a pediatrician's office in Jackson Heights. It's a great place and I get to do what I love most, which is to be around kids. I don't have any of my own, so for me it is great. I try to keep them calm and entertained so they don't cry. I play with them, read them stories...all this in between answering the phones and making appointments. It's really busy, but most of the time it's a lot of fun!"

Create your own speech and then practice it with friends and family until you feel comfortable.

NETWORKING IN PRACTICE

Besides knowing who you are and what your goals are, to strengthen your networking abilities, it is also important to know all those things you can offer to people you will be meeting. By completing this questionnaire, you will have—all in one place—everything you can share every time you meet someone new.

■ Write down your areas of knowledge and expertise (things you know well).

_____

_____

_____

_____

■ Make a list of key people you know and you have access to.

_____

_____

■ Make a list of inside information you have access to (it could be when the new fall collection will hit the stores where you work, which gives shoppers a heads up; or you might know about openings in your company).

_____

_____

■ Make a list of organizations that you have access to (professional organizations, clubs, etc.).

_____

_____

■ Make a list of things you have access to (it could be financial capital, free meeting space, etc.).

_____

_____

INDEX

ABOUT THE AUTHORS

Mariela Dabbah is the author of *Cómo Conseguir Trabajo en los Estados Unidos, Guía Para Latinos* and *Ayude a Su Hijo a Tener Éxito en la Escuela, Guía Para Padres Latinos*, both published by Sourcebooks. She was featured in "All Things Considered" (NPR), "Despierta América" (Univision), "Cada día con María Antonieta" (Telemundo), "Directo desde EEUU" (CNN en Español), "Exclusiva" (ABC News), and many other television programs, radio shows, and newspapers.

She received her MFA from the University of Buenos Aires and has lived in the U.S. since 1988. She was the owner of *Flame*, an educational book company where she developed manuals and educational training programs for teachers and parents. Since 2000, she has been focusing on her career as a writer and speaker, presenting at corporations and educational organizations. She is a contributor for Hora Hispana by the *New York Daily News,* and along with Mr. Poiré, writes a monthly column for *Tú dinero* magazine. Ms. Dabbah is also a fiction writer. Her book Cuentos de Nuevos Aires y Buena York was published in Argentina by Editorial Metafrasta in 2005. She writes and presents both in Spanish and in English.

Contact Ms. Dabbah by email at **mariela@marieladabbah.com**.

Arturo Poiré is a Senior Human Resources Executive at a major global financial services corporation. In this capacity, he has carried out assignments in South America, the UK, and Asia in the areas of merger integration, reorganization, change management, talent management, and strategic staffing. He has also done extensive work in career and executive coaching.

Mr. Poiré has a degree in Sociology from the Social Sciences School of the University of Buenos Aires and an MBA from New York University—Stern School of Business. As a sociologist, his work focused on organizational dynamics, including change management and communication strategies, and the impact of democracy on the educational system. He has collaborated with newspaper articles on cultural and social topics. He has lived in New York since 1996.

Contact Mr. Poiré by email at **arturo@thelatinoadvantage.com**.